DAO Governance in Theory and Practice

Andrea Cesaretti

DAO Governance in Theory and Practice

Metrics, Cases, and Structural Evaluation for Decentralized Autonomous Organizations

palgrave
macmillan

Andrea Cesaretti
Rimini, Italy

ISBN 978-3-032-09674-6 ISBN 978-3-032-09675-3 (eBook)
https://doi.org/10.1007/978-3-032-09675-3

This Palgrave Macmillan imprint is published by the registered company Springer Nature Switzerland AG.
The registered company address is: Gewerbestrasse 11, 6330 Cham, Switzerland

Preface

This book was conceived at the intersection of research, professional practice, and intellectual exploration. Over the past two decades, I have observed how the promises of decentralization, transparency, efficiency, disintermediation, repeatedly collide with the complex realities of governance. From early blockchain experiments to the proliferation of decentralized autonomous organizations (DAOs), the recurring question has been whether algorithmic coordination can truly replace, or at least complement, traditional forms of institutional trust.

The motivation for writing this book was twofold. First, I felt that debates around DAOs were often polarized: either narrowly technical, focused on protocols, or purely philosophical, detached from practice. My aim has been to bridge this gap, offering an exploration both theoretically rigorous and empirically grounded. Second, I wished to bring together insights from political theory, economics, computer science, and organizational studies to highlight how DAOs are not merely technical artifacts but cultural, institutional, and epistemological experiments.

While the chapters follow a deliberate progression, from diagnostics and metrics to philosophical reflections and design proposals, this volume should also be read as a personal journey. It reflects an attempt to reconcile two commitments: the search for clarity through conceptual frameworks and the recognition that governance, especially in decentralized contexts, is inevitably shaped by ambiguity, dissent, and collective memory.

This work has been enriched by exchanges with scholars, developers, and policymakers, whose insights and critiques have challenged assumptions and inspired refinements. Any shortcomings remain entirely my own.

Finally, I wish to underline the personal dimension of this endeavor. Writing about governance is always, in some sense, writing about responsibility, towards communities, institutions, and ideas. This book is dedicated to those who see decentralization not merely as code, but as a collective experiment in responsibility: the aspiration to govern together with fairness, resilience, and imagination.

Competing Interests The author is the founder of EmpowerX, an early-stage DAO-based project. This affiliation had no influence on the research design, analysis, or conclusions presented in this book. The author declares no other competing interests relevant to the content of this work.

Contents

About the Author

Andrea Cesaretti is an independent scholar specializing in decentralized finance, blockchain governance, and financial innovation. With over three decades of professional experience as a certified public accountant and statutory auditor, he has combined practice with research, focusing on the legal and economic implications of emerging technologies.

He has taught Business Administration and later Technological Finance at the Catholic University of Milan, where he developed courses and seminars on digital finance and organizational transformation. His research covers token economics, DAO governance frameworks, and the systemic risks of decentralized finance.

His previous works include La moneta complementare locale: Studio per la moneta locale di un comune italiano (2021), which examines the design of complementary currencies, and Bitcoin. Il denaro che non ubbidisce (2019), which analyzes the political and monetary implications of cryptocurrencies. He is also co-author, with Roberto Moro Visconti, of Digital Token Valuation (Palgrave Macmillan 2022).

Through his academic writing and professional activity, Cesaretti contributes to the development of transparent, resilient, and human-centered governance models for the digital economy.

List of Figures

List of Tables

CHAPTER 1

Introduction

1.1 Origins and Foundational Principles of DAOs

Decentralized autonomous organizations (DAOs) represent a novel form of institutional coordination emerging from the intersection of blockchain technology, economic incentive design, and distributed governance. At their core, DAOs are software-mediated organizations in which rules, procedures, and decision-making processes are encoded in smart contracts, self-executing code deployed on decentralized networks such as Ethereum. Unlike traditional firms or associations, DAOs operate without centralized leadership or legal incorporation, relying instead on token-based voting systems, public ledgers, and open participation to coordinate action.

The term DAO was first popularized by Vitalik Buterin (2014), who envisioned them as "companies that run themselves," capable of executing collective goals through predefined logic, without managerial oversight. However, the idea of autonomous coordination dates back further, intersecting with cypherpunk visions of self-organizing systems (Szabo, 1997) and Hayekian notions of spontaneous order in economic systems.

Historically, the first major implementation of a DAO was "The DAO" in 2016, an ambitious decentralized venture fund built on Ethereum. Despite its technical sophistication, The DAO was famously exploited due to a recursive call vulnerability, leading to the infamous Ethereum

A. Cesaretti, *DAO Governance in Theory and Practice*,
https://doi.org/10.1007/978-3-032-09675-3_1

hard fork. This incident sparked critical debate over whether "code is law" (Lessig, 1999) could suffice as a governance principle, and exposed the inherent limitations of purely formal systems for collective decision-making.

Since then, DAOs have evolved into a diverse and rapidly growing ecosystem, encompassing grant-making entities (e.g., Gitcoin), DeFi governance (e.g., MakerDAO, Aave), NFT-based communities (e.g., Nouns DAO), and experimental models of digital sovereignty (e.g., CabinDAO, Krause House). Their growing relevance stems from their promise to redefine organizational design, enabling more transparent, inclusive, and programmable forms of governance.

Yet, DAOs also challenge conventional theories of institutions, raising questions about legitimacy, identity, decision-making, and power. Scholars have begun to analyze DAOs as digital institutions (Reijers et al., 2022), networked commons (Schneider, 2022), and hybrid socio-technical systems (Wright & De Filippi, 2015). As these organizations mature, the need for theoretical frameworks and empirical tools to assess their institutional health becomes more urgent.

To understand their transformative potential, as well as their limitations, it is essential to examine how DAOs operationalize these principles in practice.

Decentralized autonomous organizations (DAOs) emerged as an attempt to reconfigure how collective decisions are made, leveraging blockchain infrastructures to reduce reliance on centralized authority and trusted intermediaries. At their core, DAOs encode organizational rules into smart contracts and employ distributed voting systems to reach consensus, enabling forms of cooperation that are theoretically transparent, tamper-resistant, and borderless.

The conceptual genealogy of DAOs intersects with several traditions: cybernetics and systems theory, which emphasize feedback loops and self-regulation; game theory, which informs incentive design in permissionless environments; and political theories of distributed governance, such as those advanced by Ostrom's work on polycentric institutions. DAOs are thus not merely technical artifacts but institutional experiments, shaped by foundational tensions between automation and deliberation, individual stake and collective will, openness and accountability.

While the collapse of "The DAO" in 2016 exposed severe vulnerabilities, it also marked the beginning of a broader experimentation process. Today's DAOs span a wide spectrum, from protocol-level

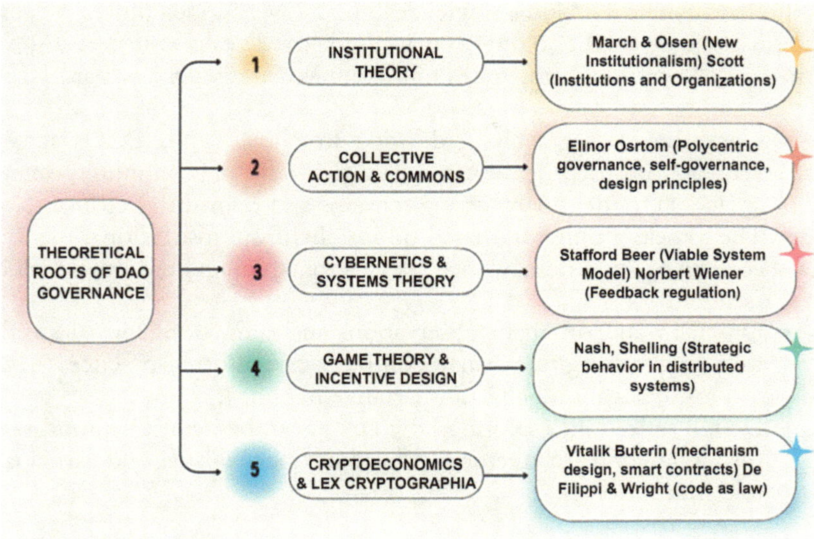

Fig. 1.1 Theoretical Roots of DAO Governance

governance (e.g., MakerDAO) to community-centric initiatives (e.g., Nouns DAO) to hybrid organizations combining on-chain and off-chain structures. This diversity reflects both the flexibility and the fragility of the model, which continues to evolve in response to legal, technical, and cultural pressures.

To contextualize the intellectual landscape that informs DAOs, Fig. 1.1 maps key theoretical lineages across disciplines. From institutional theory to cybernetics, from political science to economic sociology, DAOs emerge at the intersection of normative aspirations and formal constraints.

1.2 Objective of the Study and Methodological Approach

This book aims to critically investigate the design, limitations, and epistemological underpinnings of DAOs, framing them as socio-technical institutions that combine algorithmic coordination with emergent governance dynamics.

Rather than prescribing a single ideal model, we adopt a pluralistic and interdisciplinary methodology to map the layered realities of DAO governance. The approach integrates four complementary perspectives:

- Comparative case analysis, drawing from real-world DAOs across verticals (protocol governance, grant allocation, community management) to identify recurring tensions and reform trajectories;
- Theoretical grounding, based on insights from institutional theory, collective action frameworks, systems thinking, and incentive design (see Fig. 1.1);
- On-chain and off-chain observation, analyzing both formal structures (e.g., voting rules, smart contracts) and informal practices (e.g., forums, delegation behavior, narrative framing);
- Design reflection, exploring how DAOs can be iteratively improved through hybrid architectures, procedural mechanisms, and participatory innovations.

This multi-angle framework allows us to assess DAO governance not only by its outputs, but by its evolving structure, internal legitimacy, and capacity to sustain collective intelligence over time. Each chapter builds on this foundation, addressing a different dimension: from governance reforms and measurement (Ch. 2–5) to design patterns (Ch. 6), epistemological limits (Ch. 7–8), and philosophical implications (Ch. 9–10)

1.2.1 *Recurring Challenges in DAO Governance*

Despite their promise of greater equity, transparency, and participation, many DAOs experience systemic dysfunctions that undermine their decision-making capacity and long-term sustainability. These challenges are not marginal anomalies but reflect structural limitations in the models currently in use.

The following section analyzes the main issues that have emerged in the practical functioning of DAOs.

1.2.2 *Anonymity and Conflicts of Interest*

The permissionless and pseudonymous architecture of DAOs enables open participation but makes it difficult to identify economic or personal ties between voters and the projects under deliberation. This opens the door to undisclosed conflicts of interest, particularly during the approval of financial or resource allocation proposals.

The absence of formal disclosure mechanisms reduces the substantive transparency of the process and can lead to opaque forms of self-dealing or favoritism.

1.2.3 Power Concentration and Whale Domination

Most DAOs adopt voting systems that are proportional to the number of tokens held. While this model aligns with the logic of *skin in the game,*[1] it results in a concentration of decision-making power in the hands of a few large holders (the so-called whales), who can heavily influence voting outcomes.

This creates a structural tension between democratic principles and market logic, with the risk that governance may evolve into a token-based oligarchy.

1.2.4 Decision Overload and Deliberative Ineffectiveness

The horizontal decision-making model of DAOs can lead to a proliferation of proposals, updates, voting requests, and technical discussions. In the absence of thematic filters, effective moderation, or role differentiation, the system can become congested.

The community may be asked to vote on highly specialized topics without possessing the necessary expertise, resulting in ineffective or arbitrary decisions.

1.2.5 Low Participation and Stakeholder Apathy

Many DAOs exhibit extremely low active participation relative to the total number of token holders. The lack of meaningful incentives, the technical complexity of voting tools, and the cognitive fatigue associated with frequent decisions contribute to a phenomenon of voting apathy.

[1] Skin the Game: Anglo-Saxon expression that indicates a person's direct involvement in a decision or initiative through their own means or financial risk. In the context of DAOs, it refers to the idea that those who hold more tokens, and therefore have more "at stake," should have greater decision-making power.

In some cases, the minimum quorum is not reached; in others, decisions are made by a marginal minority, resulting in a loss of legitimacy.

1.2.6 Social Influence, Informational Asymmetries, and Manipulation

In contexts lacking moderation or accountability, voting processes can be swayed by orchestrated campaigns, strategic endorsements, or biased narratives. The informational asymmetry between expert proposers and general voters undermines the fairness of deliberative processes.

Furthermore, the ability to shape perception through social channels or proposal aggregators (e.g., Discord, Snapshot) introduces dynamics that reduce substantive transparency, even when formal on-chain traceability is preserved.

1.2.7 Symbolic Governance and "DAO in Name Only"

In many projects, the DAO structure is adopted for marketing or legitimacy purposes, but actual decisions are made by a central team or a small *multisig* group. In such cases, participation is limited to secondary or advisory votes, while strategic decisions are concentrated elsewhere, undermining the principles of decentralization and participatory governance driven by top-down logic. This phenomenon, also referred to as *governance washing*,[2] undermines the coherence between the declared architecture and the actual governance structure.

1.2.8 Legal Ambiguity and Lack of Accountability

DAOs often operate without a recognized legal form, making it difficult to determine liability in cases of disputes, fraud, or regulatory violations. In many jurisdictions, a DAO is treated as an unregistered association or de facto entity, which has significant implications for the personal liability of its participants.

The absence of a clear legal framework creates uncertainty for both internal members and third parties interacting with the organization.

[2] Expression used to describe the phenomenon in which a DAO adopts a façade of decentralization while retaining centralized control over operational decisions.

1.3 Case Studies and Comparative Analysis

Observing real-world cases allows the theoretical analysis to be enriched with empirical evidence on the structural limitations of DAOs. The following examples, selected from among the most emblematic in the Web3 landscape, highlight various types of dysfunction, from technical vulnerabilities to the fragility of internal governance.

This foundational episode, though unique in its historical impact, anticipated many of the structural challenges that will be analyzed through real-world case studies in Chaps. 2 and 3.

1.3.1 The DAO (2016): Systemic Failure and Hard Fork

The case of "The DAO" represents the original archetype of the decentralized autonomous organization concept. Launched in 2016 as a collective investment fund on Ethereum, The DAO raised over $150 million in ETH before falling victim to a cyberattack that exploited a vulnerability in its smart contract.

The resulting loss of funds and the controversial decision to execute an Ethereum *hard fork*[3] to restore them highlighted two fundamental issues: the lack of adequate pre-deployment audits and the DAO's inability to respond swiftly to critical events.

This case illustrates the tension between automation and corrective capacity, as well as the challenge of accountability within pseudo-autonomous environments.

1.3.2 Aragon: Internal Fractures and an Unfinished "Exit-to-community"

Aragon, a platform designed to build modular DAOs, experienced deep internal crises despite its strong ideological commitment to decentralization. After years of centralized development, the project attempted an *"exit-to-community,"*[4] transferring control to the DAO.

[3] Radical change to a blockchain protocol that creates an irreversible split in the network, resulting in two incompatible versions. It can be used to fix errors, introduce new rules, or, as in the case of "The DAO," to reverse an event deemed critical.

[4] Exit strategy in which the founders or initial team of a project relinquish operational control and governance to the community, transforming the organization into a DAO. The

However, a lack of cohesion among members, conflicts between the core team and the DAO, and difficulties in treasury management led to decision-making paralysis and operational breakdown.

The Aragon case illustrates that transitioning from corporate governance to decentralized governance requires more than structural changes—it demands a cultural, operational, and trust-based fabric that is often underestimated.

1.3.3 SushiSwap: Leadership, Fork, and "De Facto Centralization"

SushiSwap was launched as a *fork*[5] of Uniswap with the aim of creating a more decentralized DEX. However, strong personalistic leadership dynamics emerged within the first months, culminating in the withdrawal of the founder ("Chef Nomi") and the subsequent takeover by new technical teams.

Despite the appearance of DAO governance, many strategic decisions were made by small multisig groups or informal circles without accountability mechanisms to the broader community.

This case highlights the difficulty of building truly distributed governance when faced with urgent operational needs and a weak collective identity.

1.3.4 Snapshot-only DAOs: The Illusion of Liquid Democracy

Many modern DAOs use Snapshot as an off-chain voting tool, leveraging its ease of use and compatibility with ERC-20 token ownership. However, relying exclusively on Snapshot, without delegation systems, adaptive quorums, or deliberative filters, often results in unrepresentative decisions marked by low participation rates and vote concentration.

Moreover, the non-binding nature of off-chain voting leads to a mostly consultative form of governance, where the value of the vote depends on the goodwill of technical administrators.

goal is to achieve effective decentralization, though the transition often involves coordination and legitimacy challenges.

[5] Technical term indicating a split in the code or blockchain. It can create a new version of the original project, either compatible (soft fork) or incompatible (hard fork), for purposes of development, bug fixing, or expressing dissent within the community.

Although widespread, this model tends to produce weak and easily bypassed governance.

Cross-Case Analysis
Despite contextual and technological differences, the analyzed cases converge around several common critical issues:

- The asymmetry between declared governance and actual governance;
- The absence of structured barriers to concentrated power;
- The difficulty of reconciling participatory openness with executive capacity;
- The lack of formal accountability in the absence of legal recognition.

These factors suggest the need for design solutions that go beyond merely delegating power to token holders, and instead build mechanisms that balance democratic legitimacy, technical competence, and institutional responsibility.

1.4 Mitigation Strategies and Mechanisms

In light of the recurring issues observed in DAO models, this section proposes a set of conceptual and operational tools to mitigate the most significant systemic risks. The strategies outlined do not represent a one-size-fits-all model but rather a repertoire of adaptable solutions, depending on the nature, scale, and objectives of the decentralized organization.

1.4.1 Liquid Delegation and Delegation Councils

Liquid delegation allows participants to transfer their voting power to a trusted representative while retaining the ability to revoke it at any time. This mechanism introduces a flexible form of representation, useful for enhancing deliberative quality, reducing participatory apathy, and rewarding competence.

Some DAOs implement thematic delegations or establish formal or reputation-based "delegation councils," which play an advisory or operational role, acting as intermediaries between the broader community and the executive multisig.

1.4.2 *Reputation Systems and Penalties for Opportunistic Behavior*

A governance system based solely on token ownership is vulnerable to speculative dynamics and opportunistic behavior. The introduction of reputation-based metrics, derived from contribution levels, voting quality, community engagement, or peer approval, can promote the meritocratic selection of participants. Some advanced models include *slashing*[6] mechanisms or reputational penalties for those who abuse the governance process or act with conflicts of interest.

1.4.3 *Thematic Voting and Adaptive Quorum*

Decision-making fragmentation and deliberative overload can be mitigated by dividing the process into thematic sections, each with specialized delegates and differentiated quorum thresholds. Adaptive quorum biasing adjusts the required threshold for vote validity according to the significance and risk level of the proposal, preventing complex decisions from being approved by a residual minority.

This mechanism supports a modular and contextualized form of governance that balances efficiency with legitimacy.

1.4.4 *Distributed Moderation and Pre-vote Filtering*

The quality of the deliberative process can be enhanced through curation systems in which proposals must pass a preliminary validation phase, either formal or informal. Moderators, either elected by the DAO or selected based on reputation criteria, can perform filtering functions, thematic aggregation, compliance checks, or requests for clarification. If well structured, this step reduces informational noise and helps prevent poorly defined or strategically manipulative proposals from reaching the vote.

1.4.5 *Hybrid Models: DAO + Technical Committees*

Combining community-based governance with technical bodies (such as expert committees, operational teams, or small boards) can improve decision-making effectiveness without sacrificing transparency.

[6] Penalty mechanism in some DAOs or proof-of-stake blockchains that involves the loss of funds by those who violate governance or consensus rules.

These committees may serve an instructive, evaluative, or advisory function, while final decisions remain in the hands of the DAO.

This hybrid model is especially useful in high-complexity contexts such as DeFi protocols, treasury management, or investment evaluation.

Transparency in appointments and post hoc accountability remain key elements to prevent centralizing drift.

1.4.6 Internal Arbitration: Decentralized Dispute Resolution Models

In the absence of recognized legal status, DAOs can implement internal systems for resolving disputes based on community voting, on-chain juries, or dedicated decentralized arbitration protocols (e.g., Kleros).

While these systems do not carry binding legal authority, they enhance internal cohesion and trust in governance.

The introduction of clear procedural rules, defined timelines, and separated roles between proposers, arbitrators, and voters is essential for the legitimacy of the process.

1.4.7 Incentives for Quality Participation

To counteract participatory apathy and encourage active engagement, many DAOs introduce rewards for active voters, successful proposers, or valuable contributors.

However, such incentives must be carefully calibrated to avoid unintended consequences like opportunistic voting or *governance farming*.[7] Retroactive systems based on performance or collective evaluation, rather than automatic rewards, appear more effective in fostering sustainable and high-quality participation.

[7] Expression referring to the practice of participating in DAO votes or other governance activities solely to earn rewards, without genuine interest in the outcome or the quality of the contribution. This behavior is considered opportunistic and potentially harmful to the integrity of the decision-making process.

1.5 Toward a Sustainable Framework for DAO Governance

The evolution of the DAO concept requires careful reflection not only on technical tools but, more importantly, on principles of organizational design and mechanisms of adaptation.

Effective decentralized governance must balance openness and selectivity, transparency and confidentiality, and automation and human judgment.

This section outlines a set of guiding principles for a design framework aimed at ensuring the long-term sustainability of DAOs.

1.5.1 *Criteria for Resilient and Evolutionary Design*

A sustainable DAO must also be capable of evolving and improving over time through trial, adaptation, and interaction with its environment. This requires the design of a system that is:

- Modular, where components (voting, proposal, execution) are separable and upgradable;
- Observable, with internal audit systems and traceability not only on-chain but also at the deliberative and reputational level;
- Adaptive, able to incorporate cyclical mechanisms of review and learning within the governance process.

Special attention should be given to change management by including mechanisms for rule updates (e.g., "constitutional amendments") via enhanced quorums or multi-level processes.

1.5.2 *Balancing Openness, Effectiveness, and Accountability*

Openness is a foundational principle of DAOs, but it cannot be treated as absolute. A sustainable framework must integrate:

- *Progressive access systems*, where influence grows based on commitment, reputation, or contribution;
- *Informed delegation models*, allowing differentiated participation based on interest and expertise;

- *Distributed accountability mechanisms*, where every role, whether formal or emergent, is traceable, assessable, and potentially replaceable.

The adoption of ethical codes, internal transparency policies, and behavioral guidelines within the DAO can further strengthen collective responsibility, even in the absence of a formal legal structure.

1.5.3 Guidelines for Long-term Resilient DAOs

Based on the preceding analysis, the following concise guidelines are proposed for designing operational and enduring DAOs:

- Separation of functions: Distinguish between deliberative, technical, and executive roles, assigning clear and verifiable responsibilities to each.
- Substantive transparency: Beyond on-chain traceability, ensure the availability of public documentation, voluntary disclosures, and accessible summaries of proposals.
- Distributed control: Avoid the concentration of power in multisigs or core teams managing the treasury by implementing role rotation or supervisory committees.
- Meaningful participation: Reward not merely activity (e.g., number of votes cast), but the quality of contributions through reputational or retroactive incentives.
- Self-correction mechanisms: Include audits, constitutional reviews, emergency committees, and regular policy review processes.
- Progressive integration with the external world: Build bridges to recognized legal structures only when necessary, while preserving the DAO's inherently decentralized nature.

The proposed framework does not aim to replace existing models but to offer a conceptual foundation for experimental design in post-bureaucratic organizational forms. DAOs should neither emulate traditional corporate models nor disregard the demands for reliability, traceability, and adaptability that every sustainable organization must address.

1.6 Final Reflections

Decentralized autonomous organizations represent one of the most ambitious attempts to reimagine collective governance in the post-institutional era.

Born out of a desire to overcome the inefficiencies and asymmetries of traditional organizations, many DAOs have encountered structural challenges that call into question their actual ability to operate fairly, transparently, and sustainably.

The analysis presented in this chapter shows that the problems facing DAOs stem not so much from a lack of technology, but from still-immature institutional design.

The challenges of qualified participation, flexible representation, substantive transparency, and collective accountability cannot be addressed by technical tools alone, they require deep reflection on organizational models and the principles of governance being adopted.

Nevertheless, DAOs continue to offer an unprecedented laboratory for social innovation. Their ongoing experimentation represents a unique opportunity to explore new balances between automation and deliberation, between code and culture, between efficiency and inclusivity.

1.7 Future Research and Methodological Perspectives

The emerging nature of DAOs makes comparative approaches, empirical documentation, and longitudinal analysis of governance models essential. Future research could focus on:

- Measuring the impact of implemented governance reforms (e.g., dynamic quorum, delegated voting, reputation systems);
- Exploring the interaction between DAOs and national or supranational regulations, with particular attention to the European post-MiCAR context;
- Designing institutional health indicators to assess the long-term sustainability of DAOs;
- Studying the cultural and behavioral dynamics that emerge in decentralized environments beyond their technical components.

Finally, the unresolved question of hybridizing radical decentralization with formal accountability remains a promising field of inquiry, one that may redefine not only DAO governance but the very concept of organization in the digital age.

1.8 Insight Takeaways: Foundational Challenges in DAO Governance

1. Token-weighted voting is not neutral

While aligned with "skin in the game" logic, it risks turning DAOs into plutocracies dominated by whales, undermining inclusivity.

2. Transparency ≠ Accountability

On-chain traceability does not guarantee actual responsibility when decision-making is concentrated in multisigs or informal circles.

3. Participation without moderation leads to overload

Proposal congestion, decision fatigue, and deliberative inefficacy are recurring problems in flat governance systems.

4. Decentralization can be symbolic

The DAO label is sometimes used as a form of governance-washing, where power remains in centralized or opaque structures.

5. Legal ambiguity weakens legitimacy

The lack of formal recognition complicates liability, enforcement, and trust among participants and external stakeholders.

6. Governance is also cultural

Decentralization requires not only technical tools but also shared norms, operational cohesion, and collective trust dynamics.

References

Buterin, V. (2014). *DAOs, DACs, DAs and More: An incomplete terminology guide*. Ethereum Foundation Blog. https://ethereum.org/en/blog/2014/05/06/daos-dacs-das

Lessig, L. (1999). *Code and other laws of cyberspace*. Basic Books.

Reijers, W., Wiertz, C., & Hassan, S. (2022). Now that we have a DAO, what's next? *Patterns*, *3*(5), 100499.

Schneider, N. (2022). *Governable spaces: Democratic design for online life*. Verso Books.

Szabo, N. (1997). Formalizing and securing relationships on public networks. *First Monday*, *2*(9), https://firstmonday.org/ojs/index.php/fm/article/view/548

Wright, A., & De Filippi, P. (2015). *Decentralized blockchain technology and the rise of lex cryptographia*. SSRN. https://ssrn.com/abstract=2580664

CHAPTER 2

From Principles to Practice: Measuring the Impact of Governance Reforms in DAOs

2.1 Introduction

This chapter outlines a structured taxonomy of recurring challenges affecting DAO governance, laying the groundwork for the case analysis and mitigation strategies that follow.

In recent years, decentralized autonomous organizations (DAOs) have emerged as a new paradigm for collective coordination, aiming to replace traditional hierarchical structures with distributed and transparent governance mechanisms. Driven by the promise of increased inclusivity, accountability, and direct participation, many DAOs have experimented with innovative forms of voting, deliberation, and resource allocation (Buterin, 2014). However, as discussed in the previous contribution "Beyond the Promise of Decentralization," adopting decentralized models does not automatically guarantee the effectiveness, legitimacy, or sustainability of decision-making processes.

In response to these challenges, many DAOs have initiated internal reforms to improve governance quality by introducing mechanisms such as dynamic quorum, delegated voting (liquid delegation), and reputation systems. While the experimental phase has sparked considerable design enthusiasm, measuring the actual impact of such reforms remains largely unexplored or insufficiently systematized (Hsieh et al., 2018).

A. Cesaretti, *DAO Governance in Theory and Practice*,
https://doi.org/10.1007/978-3-032-09675-3_2

How can we assess whether an adaptive quorum truly improves participation or prevents distorted voting outcomes? What is the balance between efficiency and power concentration in a fluid delegation system? How does a reputation system influence the quality of approved proposals or the legitimacy perceived by community members?

This work aims to address these questions by proposing a methodological framework for assessing the impact of governance reforms in DAOs. The goal is not to define an ideal model, but to provide practical tools to understand whether, and to what extent, the introduced innovations produce measurable and desirable effects. The adopted perspective is multidisciplinary: it combines theoretical analysis, quantitative indicators, on-chain observation, and comparative case studies.

Only through rigorous and transparent impact measurement can we distinguish true innovation from marketing, and genuine participation from a mere democratic façade.

2.2 Governance Reforms in DAOs: A Conceptual Overview

The original promise of DAOs, distributed, transparent, and participatory governance, has revealed structural limitations in practice (Hassan et al., 2021). To address these, many decentralized organizations have initiated internal reforms that go beyond technical innovation and aim to rethink the design of collective deliberation. This chapter offers a classification of the main reforms implemented, clarifies their underlying logic, and anticipates the main impact hypotheses that will later be explored in this work through measurable indicators.

As DAOs experiment with new governance models, they also challenge traditional legal and institutional paradigms, advancing a form of lex cryptographia where code enforces norms autonomously. This concept, notably articulated by Wright and De Filippi (2015), underlines the normative shift that occurs when formal authority is embedded in programmable logic rather than in human institutions.

2.2.1 *Dynamic Quorum: Adjusting the Threshold to the Proposal's Relevance*

In most DAOs, voting is subject to a static quorum, a minimum participation threshold to validate the outcome of a proposal. However, this approach can be ineffective or prone to manipulation as it fails to account for the relevance of the decision. The dynamic quorum (or adaptive quorum) introduces a more sophisticated logic, where the required participation threshold adjusts based on factors such as:

- The amount of funds involved,
- The number of participants potentially affected by the proposal,
- The complexity or risk level of the proposal.

Impact Hypothesis: Greater legitimacy for high-impact decisions, reduced voter apathy in minor proposals, and lower risk of governance capture.

2.2.2 *Delegated Voting and Liquid Delegation: Efficiency and Representation*

Delegated voting allows DAO members to temporarily transfer their voting power to a delegate, typically based on trust, expertise, or thematic affinity.

Liquid delegation is its evolution. It allows users to:

- Delegate by thematic area (e.g., treasury, development, marketing),
- Revoke delegation at any time,
- Publicly monitor the delegate's decisions.

This model aims to increase decision-making efficiency without sacrificing legitimacy, bridging the gap between direct participation and representation.

Impact Hypothesis: Improved average decision quality, greater engagement of passive token holders, potential power concentration among "super-delegates."

2.2.3 *Reputation Systems: Merit, Trust, and Penalties*

Reputation systems are designed to assign a score to each member based on a set of observable behaviors that reflect engagement, reliability, and contribution to the community. These behaviors may include active participation in voting, the submission of initiatives that receive approval, technical input or community-driven contributions, and sustained involvement over time. By quantifying merit in this way, DAOs aim to recognize commitment and competence beyond simple token ownership.

In some implementations, reputation scores influence not only voting weight but also access to governance roles and the eligibility to submit proposals. These systems can also incorporate mechanisms for penalizing behavior that undermines collective trust, such as opportunistic voting patterns, extended inactivity, or failure to disclose conflicts of interest.

The expected impact of reputation systems includes an improvement in the quality of debate, more meritocratic governance outcomes, and the emergence of community figures who are recognized for sustained contributions. However, if poorly designed or overly rigid, such systems may also suppress dissenting perspectives or marginalize newcomers, thus reproducing the very exclusions they aim to correct (Hassan et al., 2021).

2.2.4 *Interactions and Synergies Between Mechanisms*

Governance reforms such as dynamic quorum, liquid delegation, and reputation systems are not isolated solutions. In practice, they are often combined into hybrid architectures, where each mechanism complements the others. For instance, a DAO may adopt a dynamic quorum to calibrate participation thresholds, use thematic delegation to channel expertise, and apply a reputation system to surface high-quality contributors and proposals.

These interactions can reinforce governance resilience by aligning incentives, distributing decision-making power, and filtering inputs. However, they also introduce new layers of complexity, especially when assessing the effects of individual reforms becomes difficult due to interdependencies.

Understanding these synergies is crucial. A well-designed integration can enhance inclusiveness, legitimacy, and efficiency. Poorly orchestrated combinations, on the other hand, risk producing opaque systems that are hard to audit or adjust. Measuring the impact of such layered reforms thus requires holistic evaluation methods capable of capturing the interplay between technical rules and social dynamics.

2.2.5 *Reforms in Perspective: Incremental or Transformative Innovation?*

Governance reforms in DAOs are often introduced as corrective measures, responding to specific inefficiencies or failures. However, their long-term effects may vary significantly depending on whether they are embedded into the DAO's architecture from inception or added later as reactive patches.

A mechanism introduced ex post may struggle to gain traction if it clashes with pre-existing norms, cultural expectations, or legacy power dynamics. Conversely, when integrated from the outset, the same mechanism can shape user behavior and institutional identity more effectively, becoming part of the DAO's native DNA (Wright & De Filippi, 2015).

Moreover, the impact of a reform cannot be understood purely in technical terms. The same design may produce divergent outcomes across different DAOs, depending on community engagement, internal communication, and shared values. A reputation system, for instance, may foster excellence in a collaborative environment but entrench exclusion or conformity in a conflictual or disengaged community.

For these reasons, impact evaluation must distinguish between "native" and "retrofitted" reforms and always account for the broader sociocultural context in which governance mechanisms operate.

Methodological Note: Impact assessment must distinguish between "native" DAOs (where the mechanism is integrated from inception) and "reformed" DAOs.

2.3 Impact Assessment Perspectives: What Does "Impact" Mean?

Assessing the impact of governance reforms in DAOs first requires conceptual clarity: impact with respect to what? It is not enough to observe that a DAO has implemented a delegated voting system or has reached quorum, one must ask what effects this choice has produced, for whom, and with what consequences for the overall governance process.

In this chapter, we outline the main dimensions of impact to be considered and propose an analytical framework that will later be translated into concrete indicators (KPIs) in Chap. 4.

2.3.1 Deliberative Effectiveness

One of the primary goals of governance reforms is to improve the quality of the decisions made by the DAO. This includes:

- Clarity of outcomes: Is the approved proposal implementable and understandable?
- Consistency with the DAO's strategic vision,
- Technical and financial feasibility,
- Actual implementation rate of approved proposals.

Possible measurement criteria: Average approval time, % of proposals implemented within a given timeframe, post-implementation feedback, on-chain errors, or rollbacks.[1]

2.3.2 Perceived Legitimacy and Trust in the Process

A governance system is only effective if it is perceived as fair and trustworthy. The introduction of new rules, such as dynamic quorum, delegated voting, and reputation, can strengthen trust but also raise suspicions of manipulation or exclusion.

Elements to observe:

- Trust in the neutrality of the decision-making process,
- Clarity of the rules of the game,
- Transparency ex-ante and ex-post (e.g., who voted, with what weight, and why a proposal passed),
- Mechanisms for dispute resolution or appeals.

[1] Operation that undoes or restores a previous state recorded on the blockchain. It can occur through smart contract updates or governance mechanisms that allow errors, bugs, or decisions deemed harmful to be corrected. It is a rare and controversial practice, as it contrasts with the immutability typical of the blockchain.

Tools: Surveys, sentiment analysis, tracking activity in discussion channels (Discord, forums, Snapshot comments), logs of clarification, or dispute requests.

2.3.3 *Inclusiveness and Distributed Participation*

One of the foundational goals of DAOs is to broaden participation in decision-making. However, many DAOs display very low participation rates, often concentrated among a few individuals or coordinated groups.

Key questions:

- Who is actually participating in the vote?
- Are there systemic imbalances (e.g., geographic, linguistic, technological access)?
- Do the new rules increase or reduce active participation?

Metrics to analyze: % of active wallets relative to total, geographic and stake distribution, % of proposals submitted by new members, vote concentration, and average number of votes per proposal.

2.3.4 *Sustainability and Long-Term Resilience*

A sound reform does not only produce immediate effects but also contributes to building adaptive capacity. In this sense, impact must also be assessed in terms of:

- Stability of rules (too many changes signal fragility),
- Ability to manage conflicts and disagreements,
- Continuity in active participation,
- Responsiveness to critical events or "governance crises," which represent critical stress tests for organizational adaptation in decentralized ecosystems (Hsieh et al., 2018).

Possible indicators: Number of governance mechanism changes within a given period, continuity rate among active users, emergence of significant internal conflicts, frequency of extraordinary or failed votes due to lack of quorum.

2.3.5 Balance Between Control and Openness

Each reform introduces an implicit trade-off. For example:

- Dynamic quorum can reduce speculative attacks but may exclude marginal votes,
- Delegated voting improves efficiency but risks concentration,
- Reputation systems reward active members but penalize newcomers.

Impact assessment must therefore include an analysis of the balance between control, efficiency, and openness.

Recommended approach: Mapping the "externalities"[2] introduced by each reform, counterfactual[3] evaluation, and comparison with similar DAOs that did not adopt the same measure.

2.4 Metrics and Tools for Measurement

To move from theoretical diagnosis to operational evaluation, it is essential to define observable, comparable, and ideally transparent indicators. This chapter proposes a grid of KPIs (Key Performance Indicators) associated with each reform and illustrates tools and methods for collecting them.

2.4.1 Key Performance Indicators (KPIs) for Each Mechanism

To systematically assess the effectiveness of governance reforms, each mechanism must be evaluated through dedicated metrics that reflect its operational logic, intended outcomes, and potential side effects (Choudhury & Koens, 2023).

[2] Side effects, often unintended, of a decision or reform that affect parties other than those directly involved. They can be positive (widespread benefits) or negative (harms or distortions). Mapping externalities involves identifying and assessing these indirect impacts to better understand the overall consequences of a reform.

[3] Method of analysis used to estimate the impact of a reform or decision by comparing what actually happened with what might have happened in an alternative, hypothetical scenario. In DAOs, it is often applied by comparing the evolution of a DAO that adopted a reform with that of a similar DAO that did not.

2.4.1.1 Dynamic Quorum

Dynamic quorum mechanisms adjust voting thresholds based on contextual variables such as proposal impact, risk level, or treasury exposure. Relevant indicators include:

- Weighted participation rate, calculated by comparing the tokens voted to the required quorum, segmented by proposal relevance.
- Invalidation rate of votes due to unmet quorum, before and after reform adoption.
- Quorum success rate for high-value proposals (e.g., exceeding a defined USDC threshold or percentage of treasury).
- Variation in quorum thresholds over time, relative to historical participation averages.

These KPIs help determine whether the mechanism increases responsiveness and prevents low-participation distortions without excluding marginal voters (Hassan et al., 2021).

2.4.1.2 Delegated Voting/Liquid Delegation

Delegation mechanisms aim to enhance deliberative efficiency while preserving representational legitimacy. KPIs should track both power dynamics and behavioral engagement:

- Share of delegated tokens relative to circulating supply, as a proxy for systemic trust in delegation.
- Average delegations per active wallet, indicating the density of delegation relationships.
- Power concentration among delegates, measured via Gini index or Herfindahl-Hirschman Index (HHI) (DeepDAO, 2025).
- Delegate turnover, reflecting the flexibility and accountability of the system.
- Forum and proposal engagement by delegates, to assess whether they actively participate or merely accumulate power.

These indicators reveal whether delegation produces informed governance or risks creating passive oligarchies (Choudhury & Koens, 2023).

2.4.1.3 *Reputation Systems*

Reputation systems reward consistent contribution and penalize opportunism. Their impact should be assessed on both technical performance and community perception:

- Percentage of active wallets with non-zero reputation scores, as a signal of system coverage.
- Correlation between reputation and proposal success rate, to test meritocratic alignment.
- Distribution of voting power, comparing reputation-weighted vs. token-weighted votes.
- Use of penalties, including slashing or score decay for inactivity or bad behavior.
- Community perception of fairness, via targeted surveys or post-vote feedback mechanisms (Hsieh et al., 2018).

If calibrated correctly, these systems can reinforce meritocracy and trust; if poorly designed, they risk exclusion or performative engagement.

2.4.2 *On-Chain Analytics: Wallets, Quorum, Stake, Turnout, Weighted Votes*

On-chain analytics provide objective, tamper-resistant data that are essential for evaluating governance dynamics. These tools enable DAOs to monitor participation, detect behavioral patterns, and uncover structural imbalances in voting power or representation (Hsieh et al., 2018).

Key on-chain dimensions include:

- Voting activity per wallet: Tracking who voted, how often, and on what proposals.
- Quorum achievement: Measuring the percentage of proposals reaching minimum thresholds and detecting temporal patterns (e.g., spikes during specific governance seasons).
- Stake concentration: Identifying if a small subset of wallets dominates voting outcomes (DeepDAO, 2025).
- Delegation movements: Visualizing delegation flows, including revocations and switching behavior.
- Proposal success rate: Comparing the number of approved proposals to those actually implemented or reverted.

To extract and visualize this data, several tools are commonly used:

- DeepDAO: Offers comparative dashboards across DAOs, including participation metrics, delegate rankings, and treasury analytics.
- Tally: Specializes in on-chain delegation, vote tracking, and proposal execution data.
- Snapshot: Captures off-chain votes, often used by DAOs for low-gas-cost polling.
- Dune analytics: Allows the creation of customized dashboards and queries using SQL over blockchain data.

On-chain metrics offer reliability and transparency, but must be interpreted within a broader context. They reveal what happened, but not always why—making them a necessary but not sufficient layer for governance evaluation (Choudhury & Koens, 2023).

2.4.3 *Qualitative Approaches: Sentiment, Surveys, and Perceptions*

While on-chain data provides transparency and precision, they cannot capture the subjective dimensions of governance, trust, perceived fairness, or community sentiment. These qualitative factors are often decisive in determining the legitimacy and resilience of a DAO (Hassan et al., 2021).

To assess these dimensions, DAOs increasingly rely on qualitative tools such as:

- Surveys and structured feedback: Periodic questionnaires (e.g., via Typeform or native voting interfaces) help capture user satisfaction, clarity of rules, and confidence in delegates.
- Sentiment analysis: Automated tools (e.g., AI classifiers) applied to platforms like Discord, Discourse, or Telegram detect emotional tone and opinion trends across time.
- Community interaction heatmaps: Visualization of discussions, volume, engagement, and polarity, can highlight which proposals, delegates, or mechanisms generate the most controversy or support.

These tools are especially valuable for:

- Identifying early warning signs of disaffection or governance fatigue.
- Evaluating the clarity of communication around proposals and rules.

- Measuring perceived inclusiveness and trust in the DAO's decision-making process.

However, these methods come with limitations. Responses may suffer from bias, self-selection, or social desirability effects. Dominant voices can overshadow minority views in public forums. For this reason, it is essential to triangulate qualitative insights with both on-chain behavior and off-chain organizational signals (Choudhury & Koens, 2023).

By integrating these different lenses, DAOs can develop a more holistic understanding of their governance performance, one that acknowledges not only what users do, but also how they feel and why they engage.

2.4.4 *Limitations and Risks in Measurement*

As with any indicator system, DAO measurement is subject to distortions and interpretive limitations, including:

- Quorum manipulation: Deliberately submitting proposals during low-activity periods or splitting proposals to influence results,
- Fake or automated delegation: Votes assigned to inactive or bot-controlled entities,
- Reputation inflation: Artificially boosting reputation scores without meaningful contributions, a risk highlighted in discussions of incentive misalignment and governance gaming (Kaal & Dell'Erba, 2021),
- False positives in surveys: Distorted responses due to social filtering effects, such as echo chambers where dominant opinions overshadow quieter voices.

Proposed solution in Chap. 6: adopt an integrated approach by triangulating on-chain data, off-chain information, and qualitative perceptions.

2.5 Comparative Case Studies

To fully understand the impact of governance reforms in DAOs, it is essential to observe how these mechanisms operate in practice. This section examines several prominent DAOs that have implemented advanced voting and participation tools, analyzing their objectives, outcomes, and critical challenges. Through these comparative insights, we identify key patterns of success and failure that inform the broader discussion on decentralized governance.

2.5.1 Aragon: From Crisis to Community-Driven Governance

Aragon was initially conceived as a modular platform for building DAOs, inspired by strong ideals of decentralization. After years of development under a core team, the project attempted a radical shift: handing over governance to the broader community through an "exit-to-community" process. This transition introduced on-chain voting via Aragon Voting, delegation of decision-making to a community DAO, and a "ragequit" mechanism that allowed dissenting members to exit with their share of funds.

Despite the ambition, the transition faced significant hurdles. Active participation declined, conflicts emerged between the founding team and the community, and accusations of "governance washing," where decentralization was more rhetorical than real, surfaced. Discord channels became arenas of tension, and many proposals failed due to unmet quorum. These outcomes suggest that decentralization, without a shared organizational culture and robust participatory structures, risks becoming a source of disillusionment rather than empowerment (Aragon Project, 2023; Hassan et al., 2021).

2.5.2 Gitcoin and Thematic Liquid Delegation

Originally focused on funding open-source projects, Gitcoin evolved into a DAO to manage grants and community governance. Its governance innovations included thematic liquid delegation, where participants could assign voting power by domain, such as treasury or marketing, alongside a reputation staking system for grant reviewers and the adoption of quadratic voting to encourage more equitable resource allocation.

The results were mixed but instructive. Participation in grant rounds remained consistently high, and delegate turnover stabilized over time. However, some concerns emerged regarding favoritism in proposal selection, raising questions about transparency and the influence of reputational hierarchies. The percentage of funds allocated to proposals backed by high-reputation voters was notable, but required careful monitoring to avoid reinforcing existing power structures. Gitcoin's experience highlights how thematic delegation can enhance efficiency, provided that selection criteria and reputational mechanisms are transparent and publicly accountable (Gitcoin DAO, 2023; Choudhury & Koens, 2023).

2.5.3 Optimism: Hybrid Governance With Council and Delegates

Optimism, a DAO supporting Ethereum Layer 2 infrastructure, offers a compelling example of hybrid governance. It introduced a system combining dynamic quorum (adjusted to proposal value), vote delegation weighted by reputation, and a multisig council with authority for rapid or emergency decisions.

This model produced tangible improvements. Participation rose from 5% to 12%, delegate engagement increased, and the number of approved and implemented proposals grew by 35% within 60 days. However, debates emerged around the council's influence and the true distribution of power. Forum activity tripled following governance reforms, yet discussions continued around the balance between efficiency and decentralization. This case illustrates that hybrid structures can enhance resilience and responsiveness, but only if paired with sustained transparency and clear accountability from both delegates and council members (Optimism Collective, 2024; Messari, 2024).

2.5.4 Other Experiments: ENS, Nouns DAO, MakerDAO

Several other DAOs have adopted novel governance mechanisms, each with distinct trade-offs:

- Nouns DAO employs continuous voting via NFT auctions, sustaining high engagement and a stable funding stream. However, early centralization of NFTs posed initial challenges to equitable participation.
- ENS DAO relies on delegation and Snapshot voting, with solid engagement on technical matters, though broader participation remains limited.
- MakerDAO uses a complex structure of individual reputation systems and specialized "core units" to ensure vertical accountability. While this model supports operational depth, it has led to growing complexity and decision fatigue among participants.

These cases highlight how different mechanisms, NFT-based participation, thematic delegation, or modular governance units, can each serve strategic purposes, but must be carefully calibrated to community scale, capacity, and culture (MakerDAO Forum, 2023; ENS DAO, 2024; Nouns DAO, 2023).

2.5.5 Comparative Summary: What Works, What Doesn't, and Why

Tables 2.1 and 2.2 below synthesize the patterns observed across the case studies, comparing reforms by domain and performance.

These comparisons underscore the importance of design-context fit. The same governance mechanism may produce vastly different outcomes depending on factors such as communication strategies, community culture, and organizational maturity. In particular, successful governance reforms tend to combine technical sophistication with strong discursive transparency, inclusive deliberation processes, and clarity of roles and responsibilities.

Table 2.1 Governance mechanism testing across DAOs: effects and exposures

DAO	*Key reform*	*Observed effect*	*Highlighted risk*
Nouns DAO	Continuous voting via NFT auction	High participation and sustainable fundraising	Initial centralization of NFT
ENS DAO	Delegation + snapshot	Good participation in technical topics	Low involvement on general issues
MakerDAO	Individual reputation and core units	Operational governance with vertical accountability	Increasing complexity and management fatigue

Table 2.2 Comparative summary: what works, what doesn't, and why

Dimension	*Positive pattern*	*Recurrent frailties*
Participation	Higher with reputation staking	Rapid drop without sustained incentives
Decision Quality	Improved with thematic delegated voting	Degrades with technical proposal overload
Perceived Legitimacy	Grows with forum transparency	Collapses with opaque governance or closed multisigs
Organizational resilience	Increases with hybrid governance (DAO + team)	Fails with abrupt or poorly communicated transitions

2.6 Toward an Integrated Methodology

A serious evaluation of governance reforms in DAOs cannot rely on a single type of data. Power dynamics, legitimacy, effectiveness, and resilience emerge from complex interactions between on-chain behaviors, off-chain social dynamics, and collective perceptions. This chapter proposes a five-phase methodology that combines analytical rigor with practical adaptability, drawing on the triangulated approach suggested by Vergne (2021) and updated by Choudhury and Koens (2023).

2.6.1 *The Evaluation Triangle: Integrating On-Chain Data, Off-Chain Processes, and Perceived Legitimacy*

A rigorous evaluation framework must balance three distinct but complementary layers of analysis.

A. On-Chain Data (objective and verifiable)

Voting activity, quorum rates, delegation patterns, token distribution, proposal execution, and audit trails of governance contract changes all fall within this category.

- Advantages: Precision, transparency, repeatability.
- Limitations: Do not explain the underlying motivations or social context behind participant behaviors.

B. Off-Chain Data (organizational and social)

Includes forum discussions, governance calls, deliberation drafts, moderation dynamics, and informal practices such as multisig management.

- Advantages: Visibility into the process and cultural context for decisions. These insights illuminate procedural dynamics often missed by on-chain metrics. Qualitative, ethnographic methods can be especially useful in DAO contexts, where formal indicators often obscure informal governance (Postill & Pink, 2012).
- Limitations: Difficult to quantify, and subject to interpretive bias.

C. Perceptions and sentiment:

Covers trust in governance, perceived legitimacy, effectiveness of tools and delegates, and feedback on new rules.

- Advantages: Can anticipate trust crises and reveal emerging consensus or alienation (Vergne, 2021).
- Limitations: Susceptible to bias, polarization, or echo chamber effects.

This three-pronged framework allows evaluators to synthesize technical data with social context and interpretive feedback, offering a more holistic understanding of DAO governance. Together, these three layers form an evaluation triangle that ensures a more complete and grounded assessment of DAO governance reforms (Denzin, 1978; Jick, 1979).

2.6.2 A Five-Phase Operational Framework

Building on this triadic model, we propose a structured methodology composed of five iterative phases.

2.6.2.1 Phase 1: Scope Definition

The evaluation begins with a clear articulation of purpose. Is the aim to assess improvements in participation, deliberative quality, or legitimacy? Is the reform under review a single mechanism (e.g., dynamic quorum) or a compound system (e.g., delegated voting + reputation)? A well-defined scope ensures relevance and comparability across cases.

2.6.2.2 Phase 2: Data Collection

Data is collected from multiple sources to enable triangulation. On-chain information is gathered via tools such as Snapshot, Tally, Dune, or DeepDAO. Off-chain data is obtained through forum scraping, call transcripts, and the mapping of operational structures (e.g., multisig signers, working groups). Perception data is collected via structured surveys, ideally reaching a representative sample of ≥ 10% of active wallets, and sentiment analysis on public channels.

- On-chain: Via APIs or platforms such as Snapshot, Tally, Dune, or DeepDAO.

- Off-chain: Data scraping from forums, analysis of governance calls, mapping of community roles.
- Sentiment: Structured surveys (ideally ≥ 10% of active wallets), focus groups, or social listening tools.

2.6.2.3 Phase 3: KPI Calculation

Quantitative indicators, defined in Chap. 4, are applied to generate comparable metrics. Normalization techniques (e.g., participation relative to active users) and data visualizations (e.g., time series of quorum rates or delegation maps) help reveal underlying trends and anomalies.

2.6.2.4 Phase 4: Cross-Analysis

The most insightful results often emerge from comparing across layers. For example, a high quorum vote with low forum engagement may indicate whale-driven decision-making. Similarly, rhetoric in proposal drafts may diverge from actual behavior on-chain. Clustering participants into typologies (e.g., newcomers, superusers, passive voters) allows a more granular interpretation of governance dynamics.

- Triangulate layers: e.g., high quorum + low sentiment = whale-driven vote?
- Cluster users by engagement profile: core, peripheral, passive.
- Compare narrative framing of proposals with actual voting behavior.

2.6.2.5 Phase 5: Qualitative Evaluation and Recommendations

The final phase draws together evidence from all layers to identify recurring patterns, blind spots, and actionable recommendations. Findings are reported in a format that facilitates feedback, iteration, and institutional learning, serving both internal stakeholders and external evaluators.

2.6.3 Applicability: Small, Medium, and Complex DAOs

The proposed methodology is adaptable to DAOs of varying size and complexity. (Table 2.3)

This framework can also be employed by Web3 incubators, DAO-native investors, and independent auditors to evaluate governance maturity over time. Ideally, outputs might include:

Table 2.3 Applicability of the five-phase operational framework

Type of DAO	*Suggested applicability*
Small DAO	Focus on participation and qualitative feedback (low volume)
Medium DAO	KPI dashboard + survey + forum analysis
Complex DAO	Comprehensive framework, automated tools, periodic review

- Participation trends over the last 6–12 months
- Power concentration metrics
- Reputation-weighted proposer analysis
- Sentiment and forum engagement heatmaps
- Governance efficiency indicators (e.g., implementation lag, proposal rejection rate)

This methodology can also support DAO-native investors, accelerators, and grant providers. Outputs may include dashboards showing participation trends, voter concentration, proposal throughput, sentiment analysis, and effectiveness scores over time (Choudhury & Koens, 2023).

In short, DAO governance evaluation should evolve from intuition or isolated metrics to structured, reflexive, and transparent methodologies capable of tracking institutional health over time.

As DAOs mature, evaluation methods must mature with them, moving beyond anecdote to evidence, and beyond hype to institutional insight.

2.7 Conclusions and Recommendations

Governance reforms in DAOs are not merely technical updates, but profound interventions in the architecture of power, participation, and trust. As demonstrated in the preceding chapters, tools such as dynamic quorum, liquid delegation, and reputation systems can improve deliberative effectiveness and reduce the risk of oligarchic capture, but only if designed, communicated, and monitored carefully.

This work proposed an integrated, measurable approach to assess the impact of such reforms, combining on-chain data, social dynamics, and community perceptions. Below is a summary of key conclusions and recommendations.

2.7.1 *DAOs as Adaptive Systems: Governance as an Iterative Process*

A DAO is a continuously evolving ecosystem. Reforms must be conceived as iterative processes, not final solutions. The implementation of a new rule is not the end, but the beginning of a new cycle of learning.

2.7.2 *Checklist for DAO Designers and Independent Evaluators*

Before Implementation:

- Does the reform address a documented critical issue?
- Have the effects been simulated using historical data?
- Has the community been involved in the design?

During Adoption:

- Are dashboards and visualizations available and understandable?
- Are external audits or validations planned (including qualitative ones)?
- Have thresholds for revision or rollback been defined?

After Implementation:

- Do the KPIs show actual improvements (participation, outcomes, perceptions)?
- Has governance become more inclusive or more concentrated?
- Has the new mechanism generated unexpected side effects?

2.7.3 *For Independent Evaluators and Researchers*

- Do not limit yourself to on-chain data: integrate discursive, historical, and reputational analysis.
- Analyze both aggregate behavior and edge cases or deviant patterns.
- Adopt a digital ethnographic approach[4] to capture the cultural evolution of the DAO.

[4] Qualitative research method that studies behavior, interactions, and cultural dynamics within online communities. In the context of DAOs, it means observing forums, calls, votes, and discussions to understand emerging values, languages, roles, and conflicts as an anthropologist would in a real community.

- Compare similar DAOs with different governance choices to identify structural correlations.

2.7.4 For Investors and Internal Grant Providers in the Web3 Ecosystem (Dao-native)

- Require governance-based impact reports as part of the due diligence process.
- Prioritize projects with transparent and auditable governance architectures.
- Evaluate the community's voting behavior (real engagement or "governance washing"?).
- Support the development of open-source tools for governance evaluation.

2.7.5 Open Governance: A New Paradigm of Accountability

In a world dominated by top-down models, DAOs offer an opportunity to reimagine institutions as transparent, responsive, and built from the ground up. But this vision requires new forms of shared responsibility that go beyond voting and extend to collective stewardship of the rules of the game. The challenge of DAOs is not just technical; it is profoundly cultural. It is the challenge of reinventing how we make decisions together, beyond geographic boundaries and traditional institutions. DAOs don't just answer the question "who governs?," they especially address "how do we build trust in a network?" Designing governance that is truly participatory, and not just a hollow label, may be the most radical contribution Web3 can offer to the digital society. And the first step is to measure, with honesty and method, what works and what still doesn't.

In this sense, decentralized governance is neither a leap into the void nor anarchic utopia. It is a new form of human coordination made possible by technology but founded on rules, distributed trust, and a shared sense of responsibility.

It is not chaos, but collective intelligence.

2.8 Design Takeaways: Measuring Governance Reforms in DAOs

1. Governance innovation requires rigorous evaluation

Tools like dynamic quorum, liquid delegation, and reputation systems can improve governance, but only if their impact is measured systematically across technical, social, and perceptual dimensions.

2. Impact is multidimensional

Assess reforms not only through participation rates or proposal outcomes, but also via perceived legitimacy, inclusiveness, and long-term resilience.

3. On-chain data is not enough

Effective evaluation triangulates objective metrics, social behaviors, and community sentiment to capture the full picture of DAO governance dynamics.

4. Context matters

The same reform may produce different outcomes depending on cultural norms, adoption timing (native vs. ex-post), and communication strategies.

5. Governance is iterative

Reforms are not endpoints, but new beginnings. Their effectiveness must be monitored over time through adaptive, community-informed assessment methods.

References

Aragon Project. (2023). Aragon governance documentation. https://aragon.org/dao

Buterin, V. (2014). *DAOs, DACs, DAs and More: An incomplete terminology guide*. Ethereum Foundation Blog.

Choudhury, S. R., & Koens, T. (2023). A taxonomy of governance mechanisms in DAOs: Challenges and data-driven metrics. *Blockchain: Research and Applications, 4*(2).

Denzin, N. K. (1978). *The research act: A theoretical introduction to sociological methods* (2nd ed.). McGraw-Hill.

ENS DAO. (2024). ENS DAO governance forum. https://discuss.ens.domains/

Gitcoin DAO. (2023). Gitcoin governance hub. https://gov.gitcoin.co/

Hassan, S., Reijers, W., & Wiertz, C. (2021). Decentralized autonomous organization (DAO): Issues and challenges. *Internet Policy Review, 10*(2).

Hsieh, Y. Y., Vergne, J. P., & Wang, S. (2018). *The internal and external governance of blockchain-based organizations: Evidence from cryptocurrencies.* In Proceedings of the 51st Hawaii International Conference on System Sciences.

Jick, T. D. (1979). Mixing qualitative and quantitative methods: Triangulation in action. *Administrative Science Quarterly, 24*(4), 602–611.

Kaal, W. A., & Dell'Erba, M. (2021). *Blockchain governance and DAO regulation: Emerging frameworks* (SSRN Working Paper). https://ssrn.com/abstract=3905742

MakerDAO Forum. (2023). MakerDAO governance portal. https://forum.makerdao.com/

Messari. (2024). *Optimism governance metrics report.* https://messari.io/report

Nouns DAO. (2023). Nouns DAO governance overview. https://nouns.wtf/vote

Optimism Collective. (2024). Optimism governance documentation. https://community.optimism.io/docs/governance/

Postill, J., & Pink, S. (2012). Social media ethnography: The digital researcher in a messy web. *Media International Australia, 145*(1), 123–134.

Vergne, J. P. (2021). Decentralized governance and the challenge of legitimacy. *Oxford handbook of blockchain governance*, Forthcoming.

Wright, A., & De Filippi, P. (2015). *Decentralized blockchain technology and the rise of lex cryptographia.* https://ssrn.com/abstract=2580664

CHAPTER 3

DAO Health Framework: Designing Indicators for Long-Term Institutional Sustainability

3.1 Introduction

This chapter presents four empirical cases, chosen to highlight diverse governance challenges faced by decentralized autonomous organizations (DAOs). While grounded in specific contexts, each case reveals broader structural tensions.

In the debate surrounding DAOs, attention is often directed toward their technical or legal dimensions: smart contracts, tokenomics, quorum mechanisms, and regulatory compliance. However, many DAOs fail or become paralyzed not because of flaws in their code, but due to weaknesses in their institutional structure: the absence of organizational memory, the erosion of legitimacy, low stakeholder participation, or governance captured by a few. To assess whether a DAO is truly sustainable over time, it is essential to shift the focus from mere "activity" to "institutional vitality" that is, the organization's ability to endure, adapt, and maintain trust among its members.

3.1.1 The Difference Between Activity and Vitality

A DAO may appear active through frequent proposal submissions, on-chain transactions, and the registration of new members. Yet such activity can mask deeper pathological dynamics: internal polarization,

A. Cesaretti, *DAO Governance in Theory and Practice*,
https://doi.org/10.1007/978-3-032-09675-3_3

governance that is formally structured but operationally ineffective, high turnover rates, or the concentration of decision-making power in a few hands.

Conversely, a "healthy" DAO may operate at a slower pace but demonstrate cohesion, an ability to learn from past mistakes, and mechanisms for ongoing legitimation.

The concept of "institutional health" seeks to distinguish between apparent effervescence and true organizational resilience.

3.1.2 From Reactive Metrics to Predictive Indicators

Today, many DAO evaluations rely on superficial or retrospective metrics: the number of votes cast, assets held in the treasury, or the number of Twitter followers. Yet these indicators reveal little about a DAO's structural soundness or its long-term sustainability.

This work instead proposes a set of predictive indicators designed to offer early signals of organizational dysfunctions or latent strengths.

The goal is not to standardize DAOs into a single ideal model, but to provide analytical tools that enable a deeper understanding of their evolution as genuine institutional bodies operating within decentralized environments.

3.2 What Does "Institutional Sustainability" Mean for a DAO?

3.2.1 Beyond Treasury and Quorum

When discussing sustainability, many DAOs tend to focus on tangible elements: the size of the treasury, the minimum number of votes required to approve a proposal, or the duration of staking periods. While these aspects are certainly important, they do not fully capture the essence of institutional sustainability. A DAO may have ample financial reserves and clearly codified quorum rules, yet still be fragile, ineffective, or destined to implode. True sustainability lies in the DAO's ability to operate over time as a collective system of trust, learning, and adaptation even in the absence of a central authority.

3.2.2 *Sustainability = Adaptability + Transparency + Continuous Legitimation*

We propose to define the institutional sustainability of a DAO as the dynamic combination of three key factors:

1. Adaptability: The ability to modify rules, processes, and priorities in response to internal or external changes without compromising coherence or integrity;
2. Transparency: Not only access to on-chain data, but also the comprehensibility of decisions, rationales, and roles, : the ability to modify even for non-technical members;
3. Continuous legitimation: A process through which the DAO's decisions are perceived as fair, inclusive, and representative, not merely formally valid.

In other words, a sustainable DAO is one that succeeds in evolving without losing the trust of its members, maintaining a delicate balance between automation and human discernment.

3.2.3 *Three Fundamental Dimensions*

First, the organizational dimension reflects the structural integrity of the DAO: Are decision-making processes clearly defined? Do roles and responsibilities support operational resilience? Systems with excessive centralization or ambiguous roles risk collapse from single points of failure or conflict over legitimacy (Hassan et al., 2021).

Second, the social dimension emphasizes internal trust, relational capital, and the ability to foster participation beyond incentivized actions. DAOs, unlike traditional organizations, depend not only on code but on community dynamics. Reputation, informal leadership, and collective norms are often the true substrate of decentralized coordination (Reijers et al., 2018).

Finally, the cognitive dimension concerns the organization's ability to learn over time. Institutional memory, captured through documentation, retrospectives, and onboarding resources, acts as the connective tissue between past decisions and future evolutions. Without this, DAOs risk repeating mistakes or losing continuity amid turnover (Choudhury & Koens, 2023).

These three dimensions offer a more holistic lens through which to assess DAO sustainability, reminding us that resilience is not merely technical, but also cultural and epistemic.

3.3 Categories of Indicators

To assess the institutional health of a DAO, it is necessary to move beyond isolated metrics and develop sets of articulated and comparable indicators. The indicators we propose are organized by area, aiming to cover all fundamental dimensions, organizational, social, and cognitive, and can be adapted to the specific characteristics of each DAO. For each category, we suggest practical examples and references to patterns observed in existing DAOs.

3.3.1 Participation and Continuity

One of the key features of institutionally sustainable DAOs is their ability to maintain consistent, long-term participation from engaged members. In decentralized environments where affiliation is fluid and often informal, the mere presence of activity is not sufficient to gauge vitality. Rather, it is necessary to examine the depth, persistence, and quality of user engagement in governance processes.

A particularly useful metric in this regard is the active retention rate, defined as the percentage of wallets that have participated in at least one proposal every 30 days over a six-month period. This indicator helps differentiate between a DAO's genuinely involved community and a broader, yet more sporadically active user base.

A second relevant measure is the core-to-episodic wallet ratio, which compares the number of consistently engaged members to those who appear only during specific events—such as token airdrops, high-stakes votes, or periods of controversy. A strong core group is often associated with cohesion, continuity, and the gradual accumulation of institutional memory (Hassan et al., 2021).

Another important metric is the average engagement per proposal, which reflects the volume of interactions, comments, discussions, and votes associated with each formally submitted initiative. This measure captures not only the intensity of involvement, but also the deliberative quality of governance. High voting rates with minimal prior discussion may indicate apathy, token signaling, or procedural inefficiencies (DeepDAO, 2025; Reijers et al., 2018).

Taken individually, these indicators offer partial insights. But when analyzed in combination and over time, they help surface trends in governance health. Sustained participation is not simply a function of voting activity, it reflects whether members identify with the DAO's mission, trust its processes, and perceive their involvement as meaningful.

3.3.2 Diversity and Power Distribution

Sustainable governance in DAOs depends not only on participation volume but also on how decision-making power is distributed across the network. A decentralized system that concentrates influence in a handful of actors risks replicating the very hierarchies it seeks to avoid. Thus, evaluating diversity—across geography, language, and role distribution—and power dispersion is essential to assessing institutional health.

One of the most widely used indicators in this domain is the Gini index on voting tokens, which measures the degree of concentration in token-based voting power. A Gini coefficient approaching 1 indicates a high concentration of voting rights among a few addresses, potentially exposing the DAO to governance capture or plutocratic dynamics (Hassan et al., 2021; Choudhury & Koens, 2023). By contrast, lower Gini values typically reflect more equitable token distribution and, by extension, a broader base of potential influence.

Complementing this, geographic and linguistic diversity offers insight into the cultural and social inclusiveness of the DAO. Although often overlooked, linguistic homogeneity can hinder global participation, while geographic concentration may reflect region-specific interests rather than shared institutional goals (World Economic Forum, 2021). Tracking wallet metadata, time zones of forum activity, and language use in communication channels can help reveal hidden asymmetries in participation.

A further proxy of institutional plurality is the distribution of roles over time. This metric assesses the proportion of wallets that have taken on multiple functions—such as proposing, voting, and moderating—rather than remaining confined to a single type of participation. A DAO where a small group dominates proposal submission or discussion facilitation may experience organizational bottlenecks or reduced innovation capacity (Reijers et al., 2018).

Ultimately, diversity and power distribution metrics are not just technical indicators—they reflect the DAO's capacity to incorporate a wide range of voices, adapt to heterogeneous needs, and ensure legitimacy beyond token-weighted voting alone.

3.3.3 Execution Capacity

Voting is only meaningful if it leads to action. In many DAOs, a high volume of proposals and enthusiastic participation mask a deeper dysfunction: the inability to execute decisions effectively. A governance process that ends at voting undermines institutional credibility and diminishes long-term trust. Therefore, execution capacity—the ability to translate collective intent into concrete outcomes, is a key pillar of institutional sustainability (Reijers et al., 2018; Kaal & Dell'Erba, 2021).

A first indicator in this domain is the percentage of implemented proposals, measuring the ratio between approved initiatives and those actually enacted, whether on-chain or off-chain. A low implementation rate may suggest technical bottlenecks, lack of operational coordination, or decision fatigue. More importantly, it signals a potential disconnect between deliberation and follow-through, a phenomenon sometimes referred to as "governance theater" (Messari, 2024).

Equally significant is the average time from proposal approval to deployment, which captures the DAO's procedural efficiency. Long delays, especially in operational or grant-related decisions, may erode community trust and reduce the perceived effectiveness of the governance process. In contrast, well-defined execution pipelines (e.g., through dedicated working groups or implementation councils) often correlate with faster turnaround and clearer accountability (Choudhury & Koens, 2023).

Finally, the iteration rate on similar proposals serves as a proxy for institutional learning and responsiveness. DAOs that revisit and revise earlier decisions demonstrate a capacity for reflexivity, learning from errors or changing circumstances, rather than relying on static rulebooks. Iteration is not a sign of instability, but of adaptability and maturity (Vergne, 2021).

Together, these indicators provide a multidimensional view of whether a DAO is able to deliver on its governance promises, not just to deliberate, but to act.

3.3.4 Adaptability

A sustainable DAO must be more than just stable, it must be adaptable. In decentralized contexts where technological, regulatory, and community dynamics shift rapidly, rigid governance structures can quickly become obsolete. Adaptability, in this sense, refers to the organization's ability to evolve its rules, roles, and practices in response to both internal tensions and external shocks (Holland, 1992; Taleb, 2012).

One indicator of adaptability is the frequency of governance revisions over a given time frame (e.g., the past 12 months). Frequent, transparent revisions suggest an engaged community that responds proactively to changing needs. However, excessive changes without a clear rationale may also signal instability or a lack of strategic vision (Buterin, 2014).

Another signal is the existence and updating of a "living constitution," a foundational document that outlines the principles and procedures of governance, regularly reviewed and revised with community input. DAOs that codify their norms in this way demonstrate both institutional maturity and the capacity for reflexive governance (Wright & De Filippi, 2015; Hassan et al., 2021).

Finally, the presence of self-assessment processes, audits, and public retrospectives serves as an indicator of structured learning. DAOs that conduct periodic evaluations of their decision-making, publish "lessons learned," and invite critical reflection are more likely to adapt constructively. Such practices mirror the logic of "institutional double-loop learning" found in traditional organizations (Argyris & Schön, 1978), but updated for decentralized ecosystems.

Adaptability is not the same as volatility. Rather, it reflects an organization's capacity to change direction without losing its coherence, what Taleb (2012) describes as antifragility: systems that improve under stress. In DAO governance, this quality is essential for long-term sustainability.

3.3.5 Transparency and Accountability

Transparency is often cited as a core value of DAOs. However, the mere availability of data does not ensure genuine transparency, nor does it automatically lead to accountability. For transparency to support institutional sustainability, it must be not only technical (e.g., access to smart contract data) but also interpretive, enabling participants to understand how decisions are made, by whom, and with what rationale (Reijers et al., 2018).

An essential element is the accessibility of governance data. This includes structured, user-friendly dashboards that provide real-time information on proposals, voting outcomes, delegate performance, and treasury movements. Platforms such as Snapshot, Tally, and DeepDAO have contributed significantly to making on-chain governance more legible (DeepDAO, 2025; Tally.xyz, 2025). Yet true transparency requires that this information is not only visible, but also contextualized and comprehensible to non-expert users (World Economic Forum, 2021).

A second aspect is active reporting mechanisms. Periodic updates. Monthly or quarterly reports detailing key decisions, fund allocation, and performance indicators, serve not only informational purposes but also symbolic ones. They reinforce the perception that the organization is responsive and accountable, contributing to what March and Olsen (1984) describe as the "logic of appropriateness" in institutional behavior.

Finally, the presence of internal arbitration or appeal systems signals maturity in governance architecture. While decentralization often resists hierarchical authority, dispute resolution mechanisms, such as temporary councils, third-party mediators, or structured appeals, help manage internal tensions without escalating into forking or disengagement. These structures mirror the function of "constitutional safeguards" in traditional institutions, adapted to the flexible logic of DAO governance (Wright & De Filippi, 2015).

Transparency without accountability risks becoming surveillance. Accountability without transparency devolves into blind trust. Sustainable DAOs require both: open systems that allow scrutiny and mechanisms that respond constructively to that scrutiny.

3.4 Building a DAO Health Index (DHI)

While individual indicators provide useful insights into specific dimensions of DAO performance, they often offer only a fragmented view. To enable meaningful comparisons across different DAOs and monitor institutional evolution over time, this section proposes the construction of a composite metric: the DAO Health Index (DHI).

Rather than producing a ranking or "scoreboard," the DHI serves as a diagnostic tool, a synthetic measure capturing the overall state of institutional sustainability within decentralized organizations. The approach draws inspiration from composite indices used in development economics and governance evaluation (e.g., OECD, 2008; Esty et al., 2005), adapted to the unique features of DAOs.

3.4.1 *How to Combine Indicators Into a Composite Metric*

The construction of a robust and interpretable DHI requires a clear and replicable methodological process. The main steps include:

- Indicator selection: From the full set presented in Sect. 3.3, a representative subset is chosen (e.g., two per dimension). Selection criteria may include data availability, comparability, and relevance to the DAO's mission.
- Normalization: Each indicator must be transformed to a common scale (typically 0–100) to allow aggregation without unit-based distortion. Min–max normalization or z-score standardization may be used depending on data distribution (Nardo et al., 2005).
- Weighting: Not all indicators carry equal importance. Weighting can be set ex ante based on expert judgment, or derived ex post through statistical techniques such as principal component analysis (PCA) or factor analysis (Jolliffe, 2002). Participatory weighting, involving members of the DAO, may enhance legitimacy and contextual appropriateness.
- Aggregation: Normalized and weighted scores are aggregated into a single DHI value. Aggregation methods may vary (e.g., arithmetic mean, geometric mean) depending on whether compensation among dimensions is permitted.

The index can be further disaggregated into thematic sub-indices (e.g., DHI-Legitimacy, DHI-Execution) to support targeted diagnostics.

3.4.2 *Weighting, Benchmarking, and Longitudinal Tracking*

The analytical power of the DHI increases when contextualized through benchmarking and time-series analysis:

- Dynamic benchmarking: Scores can be compared across peer DAOs, such as grant-giving, protocol-governance, or service-oriented

DAOs, to identify sector-specific patterns and anomalies (Hassan et al., 2021).

- Temporal tracking: Periodic DHI computation allows organizations to assess the impact of reforms, identify trends in institutional maturity, or detect early signs of decline or stagnation.
- Scenario simulation: Stress-testing the DHI under hypothetical conditions—such as sudden delegate dropout, voting apathy, or treasury depletion—can offer insights into resilience thresholds and adaptive capacity.

3.4.3 *Classification Tiers: A Heuristic Tool*

To facilitate interpretation and internal communication, DHI scores can be grouped into qualitative tiers. These tiers are not intended as definitive judgments but as heuristic categories guiding strategic reflection and action.

The next table visually presents this tiered classification as a spectrum of institutional maturity. It is designed as a conversation-starter, encouraging internal review, not external competition.

As shown in Fig. 3.1, the DHI framework groups DAOs into four governance tiers. These tiers provide a simplified lens for interpreting institutional strength, highlighting different levels of systemic risk, engagement, and adaptive capacity.

This classification is purely indicative and should be understood as a tool for internal dialogue and continuous improvement, rather than as a rigid or punitive label.

Table 3.1 DHI score categorizes into qualitative tiers

Tier	*DHI score range*	*Brief description*
Dormant	0–29	Minimal activity, inactive or highly concentrated governance. High risk of collapse or hostile takeover
Active	30–59	Vibrant but unstable participation. Presence of operational discontinuities or structural weaknesses
Sustainable	60–79	Functioning structure with the ability to execute and engage. Some limitations in transparency or adaptability
Resilient	80–100	Robust governance, distributed participation, high transparency, and strong adaptive capacity

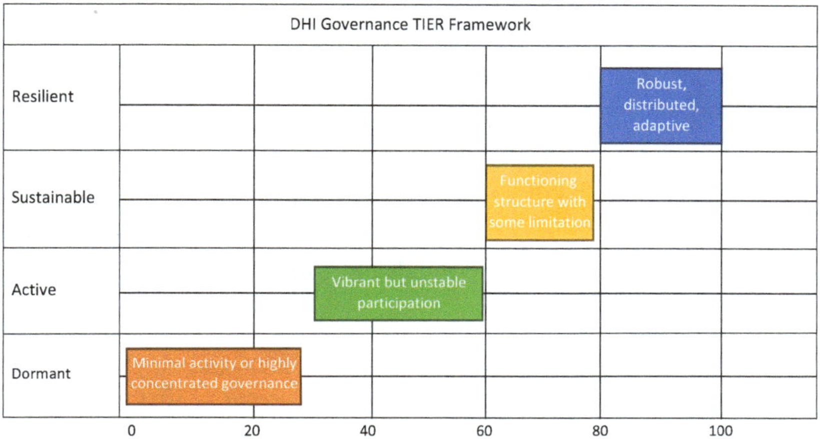

Fig. 3.1 Governance tier classification based on DHI scores. This framework categorizes DAO governance systems into four tiers based on their DHI score: Dormant (0–29), Active (30–59), Sustainable (60–79), and Resilient (80–100). Each tier reflects a distinct level of institutional health, based on participation, power distribution, adaptability, transparency, and execution capacity

3.5 Application Cases

To test the practical relevance of the DAO Health Index (DHI) introduced in Sect. 3.4, this section applies the proposed framework to three emblematic DAOs. The aim is not to provide definitive evaluations, but to illustrate how a structured set of indicators can uncover latent dynamics in governance practices, support longitudinal institutional analysis, and offer actionable insights for improvement. Rather than judging success or failure, these case studies explore how DAOs evolve under pressure, experiment with reforms, and negotiate the trade-offs of decentralization.

3.5.1 DAOs Analyzed

The case study analysis focuses on three DAOs that embody distinct governance architectures and operational logics, selected to ensure diversity in both structural design and data availability.

- Nouns DAO represents a minimal, protocol-driven model centered on NFT-based membership and continuous proposal flow via daily auctions.
- Optimism Collective offers a layered approach to governance, combining token-based on-chain voting with an appointed council empowered to act swiftly on urgent matters.
- Gitcoin DAO exemplifies a mission-driven community focused on public goods funding, integrating thematic delegation, reputation mechanisms, and iterative rounds of experimentation.

These organizations differ in scale, structure, and strategic focus, but share a commitment to exploring the boundaries of decentralized coordination. By applying the DAO Health Index across all five dimensions (participation, power distribution, execution, adaptability, and transparency), we aim to identify governance patterns and structural tensions that transcend specific use cases.

3.5.2 Interpretation of Data Over Time

The DAO Health Index (DHI) was calculated for each of the three selected DAOs using a balanced set of ten indicators, two per dimension, normalized on a 0–100 scale and equally weighted. The analysis spans at least 12 months of governance activity, allowing for both cross-sectional and longitudinal comparisons.

- Gitcoin DAO displays the highest degree of structural balance. With strong scores in participation (75), adaptability (80), and transparency (85), its governance model benefits from thematic delegation, frequent retrospective audits, and a high retention rate (45% over six months). Its power distribution (62) also improved after the introduction of delegation and reputation mechanisms.
- Optimism Collective shows high execution capacity (78), thanks to a semi-centralized council, and a substantial adaptability score (70), following the implementation of bicameral governance (Token House and Citizens' House). Its participation score (68) and transparency score (72) remain solid, though the power distribution (50) reflects concerns about latent centralization.
- Nouns DAO, while highly transparent (88), scores lower in adaptability (48) and power distribution (42), due to a persistent

concentration of governance tokens and a lack of structural evolution. The protocol's minimalist design, while innovative, shows signs of participation fatigue, as evidenced by declining engagement per proposal and high turnover rates.

These results, synthesized in Table 3.2 and visualized in Fig. 3.2, confirm that institutional sustainability is not merely a function of treasury size or proposal volume, but rather of a well-distributed, adaptive, and transparent governance architecture.

3.5.3 Pre/Post-reform Variations and Governance Evolution

The longitudinal analysis of internal governance reforms reveals how deliberate interventions can shift a DAO's institutional trajectory. Rather than focusing solely on static scores, the following insights emphasize evolutionary patterns and design responsiveness, consistent with adaptive governance literature (March & Olsen, 1984; Ostrom, 1990).

- Gitcoin DAO implemented thematic liquid delegation and reputation-weighted voting, which led to a measurable improvement in participation (+10 points) and power distribution (+8 points). These shifts pushed the DAO from the active into the sustainable tier, showcasing how incentive alignment and reputational layers can catalyze healthier governance dynamics (Hassan et al., 2021).
- Optimism Collective adopted a dual-chamber model (Token House and Citizens' House), strengthening adaptability (+15 points) and improving execution capacity. However, structural centralization persists, limiting gains in power distribution. The case illustrates the importance of pairing structural innovation with broader mechanisms of inclusion and transparency (Wright & De Filippi, 2015; Reijers et al., 2018).
- Nouns DAO, in contrast, underwent no major structural reforms. Despite high transparency, its static governance model resulted in only marginal evolution. Rising participant turnover and reduced average engagement per proposal suggest early signs of governance fatigue, a phenomenon observed in systems with weak feedback loops and limited institutional learning (Scott, 2008; Gell-Mann, 1994).

Table 3.2 Comparative DHI scores across governance dimensions for Gitcoin DAO, Optimism Collective, and Nouns DAO

DAO	*Participation*	*Power distribution*	*Execution*	*Adaptability*	*Transparency*	*Final DHI*	*Tier*
Nouns DAO	55	42	65	48	88	**59.6**	Active
Optimism Collective	68	50	78	70	72	**67.6**	Sustainable
Gitcoin DAO	75	62	70	80	85	**74.4**	Sustainable

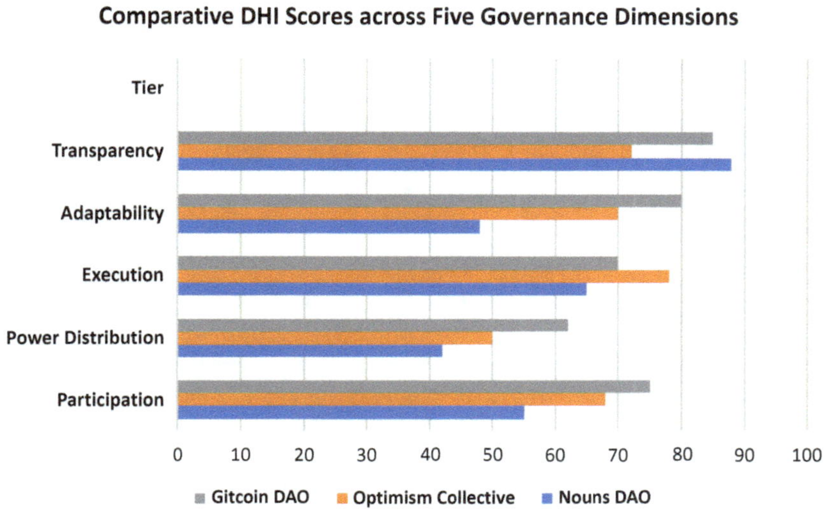

Fig. 3.2 Comparative DHI scores across governance dimensions for Gitcoin DAO, Optimism Collective, and Nouns DAO

As shown in Fig. 3.3, each DAO traces a different governance path: Gitcoin and Optimism exhibit deliberate reform cycles, while Nouns DAO relies on organic evolution, forks, and cultural shifts rather than formal institutional redesign. This divergence reinforces a central finding: institutional sustainability requires not just decentralization, but deliberate governance reflexivity.

3.6 Limitations and Future Directions

The development of the DAO Health Index (DHI) marks a significant step toward the structured evaluation of institutional sustainability within decentralized organizations. However, any measurement framework comes with inherent limitations. This section identifies critical blind spots and outlines possible trajectories for refining the model over time.

3.6.1 The Cultural Dimension: What Metrics Can't Capture

While quantitative indicators offer clarity and comparability, they inevitably fall short in capturing the full richness of institutional life. Cultural

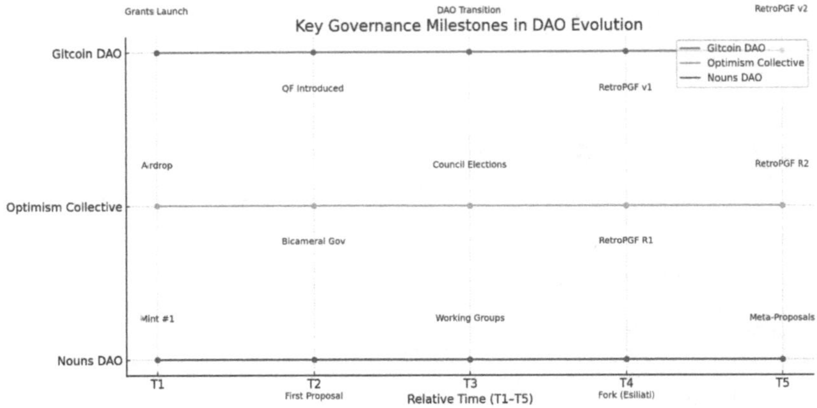

Fig. 3.3 Key governance milestones in DAO evolution. This timeline visualizes major governance-related events across three DAOs: Gitcoin, Optimism Collective, and Nouns DAO. The horizontal axis indicates relative temporal progression (T1–T5), not absolute time, and is used to compare how each organization has evolved in terms of decision-making, structure, and accountability. While Gitcoin and Optimism have adopted iterative reforms (e.g., RetroPGF rounds, bicameral governance), Nouns DAO has maintained a minimal protocol design, experiencing forks and narrative reconfigurations instead of structural governance shifts

variables, such as the degree of mutual trust, the presence of constructive dissent, or the emotional resilience of the community, remain essential yet elusive components of organizational health.

As noted in the literature on institutional sociology (Scott, 2008) and organizational ethnography (Postill & Pink, 2012), shared narratives and informal norms play a decisive role in shaping governance dynamics, particularly in decentralized systems. For instance:

- Implicit trust among participants may sustain decision-making in the absence of formal enforcement.
- Norms of deliberation affect the legitimacy and inclusivity of proposals.
- Crisis management culture influences resilience beyond codified procedures.

Future iterations of the DHI should integrate qualitative methodologies such as structured interviews, discourse analysis, and digital ethnographies to assess the "emotional temperature" and value systems of DAO communities, key aspects of what Ostrom (1990) called the "social capital" of self-governing systems.

3.6.2 *The Risk of "Cosmetic Metrics"*[1]

An often-overlooked threat in evaluation systems is the emergence of cosmetic compliance, behaviors aimed at inflating indicator scores without producing substantive improvement. This phenomenon is well documented in education (Campbell's Law) and financial regulation (Power, 1997), and may extend to DAOs as they begin to be assessed against standardized frameworks.

In such contexts, metrics lose their diagnostic power and become performative tools for external validation. DAOs might:

- Adopt superficial reforms that raise DHI scores without redistributing power;
- Increase formal transparency without enabling genuine accountability;
- Focus on measurable activity over meaningful participation.

The DHI should therefore be treated not as a competitive ranking mechanism, but as a reflective diagnostic tool, designed to support internal learning and promote long-term institutional robustness.

3.6.3 *Certification or Self-Assessment? A Strategic Choice*

As DHI-like frameworks mature, a strategic question arises: should institutional sustainability be externally certified or community self-assessed?

Two potential models can be envisioned:

- External certification: Independent evaluators or public repositories could provide governance audits, assign maturity levels, and issue

[1] "Cosmetic metrics" refer to situations where an organization modifies its practices primarily to improve the appearance of performance measures without implementing substantial changes.

"DAO sustainability scores" akin to ESG ratings or ISO standards. This could improve comparability and foster accountability, but at the risk of bureaucratization and centralization.
- Community self-assessment: Alternatively, DAOs may adopt open-source, customizable tools to periodically evaluate themselves, combining structured dashboards with deliberative reporting processes. This model preserves decentralization while fostering reflexivity and internal improvement (Choudhury & Koens, 2023).

Both approaches involve trade-offs. The former enhances credibility and external benchmarking; the latter encourages ownership and context-sensitive evaluation. In either case, the goal must remain clear: to foster institutional learning without distorting DAO autonomy.

3.7 Conclusion

The growing diffusion of DAOs marks a historic step in the experimentation with post-hierarchical organizational models. However, the concrete experience of recent years shows that technical decentralization alone is not enough: without solid institutions, without organizational memory, and without mechanisms for adaptation, many DAOs risk failure despite the efficiency of their code.

This work has proposed a systematic approach for assessing the institutional health of DAOs through a set of predictive indicators and the development of a DAO Health Index (DHI).

The aim was not to construct rankings or promote rigid standards, but to open a more mature space for dialogue around the very concept of sustainability within decentralized environments.

An index alone cannot measure everything. But it can help us ask the right questions:

- Is our DAO capable of learning from its mistakes?
- Is our governance accessible, resilient, and adaptable?
- Are we building a community that can endure beyond speculative cycles?

In the world of DAOs, true innovation lies not in on-chain voting itself, but in the ability to build trust without relying on traditional hierarchies. Healthy DAOs are those capable of aging well, evolving alongside the needs of their members, and withstanding inevitable internal and external stresses. In this sense, designing institutional sustainability is not merely a technical or organizational matter: it is a cultural challenge that demands imagination, intellectual honesty, and collective will.

3.7.1 Design Takeaways: Institutional Sustainability in DAOs

1. Sustainability goes beyond code and capital

Healthy DAOs are not defined by treasury size or voting activity, but by their ability to adapt, maintain trust, and embed collective learning.

2. Institutional vitality is multi-dimensional

Sustainability arises from the interplay of organizational structure, social cohesion, and cognitive memory, each equally vital to long-term resilience.

3. Metrics must become meaningful

DAO evaluation should evolve from superficial activity indicators to predictive diagnostics that capture deeper institutional dynamics.

4. Build for adaptability and legitimacy

Transparent governance, revisable constitutions, and continuous legitimation processes are core pillars of sustainable decentralized institutions.

5. Composite indexes are tools for dialogue, not dogma

The DAO Health (DHI) supports internal reflection and comparative analysis—but must avoid becoming a rigid ranking or cosmetic benchmark.

Acknowledgments This chapter is the result of an independent research journey that benefited from the empirical observation of numerous DAO ecosystems and critical engagement with a community of decentralized scholars, developers, and innovators.

I would like to express special thanks to analysis platforms such as DeepDAO, Snapshot, and Tally, as well as to the DAOs whose openness and transparency made it possible to access the data used in constructing the analytical models.

Heartfelt recognition is also due to all those who, through their theoretical and practical work on decentralized governance, have helped to make the debate around DAOs deeper, more rigorous, and more oriented toward sustainability.

Any errors or limitations of this contribution remain, of course, the sole responsibility of the author.

References

Argyris, C., & Schön, D. (1978). *Organizational learning: A theory of action perspective*. Addison-Wesley.

Buterin, V. (2014). *DAOs, DACs, DAs and More: An incomplete terminology guide*. Ethereum Foundation Blog. https://ethereum.org/en/blog/2014/05/06/daos-dacs-das

Choudhury, N., & Koens, K. (2023). *Measuring DAO maturity: Frameworks for reflexive governance* (DAO Research Collective Working Paper Series).

DeepDAO. (2025). DAO metrics and analytics dashboard. https://deepdao.io/

Esty, D. C., Levy, M., Srebotnjak, T., & de Sherbinin, A. (2005). *Environmental sustainability index: Benchmarking national environmental stewardship*. Yale Center for Environmental Law and Policy.

Gell-Mann, M. (1994). *The quark and the jaguar: Adventures in the simple and the complex*. W. H. Freeman.

Hassan, S., Reijers, W., & Wiertz, C. (2021). *Institutional design for DAO governance* (DAO Research Collective Working Paper Series).

Holland, J. H. (1992). Complex adaptive systems. *Daedalus, 121*(1), 17–30

Jolliffe, I. T. (2002). *Principal component analysis* (2nd ed.). Springer.

Kaal, W. A., & Dell'Erba, M. (2021). *Blockchain governance and DAO regulation: Emerging frameworks* (SSRN Working Paper). https://ssrn.com/abstract=3905742

March, J. G., & Olsen, J. P. (1984). The new institutionalism: Organizational factors in political life. *American Political Science Review, 78*(3), 734–749.

Messari. (2024). *DAO governance metrics report*. https://messari.io/report

Nardo, M., Saisana, M., Saltelli, A., Tarantola, S., Hoffmann, A., & Giovannini, E. (2005). *Handbook on constructing composite indicators: Methodology and user guide* (OECD Statistics Working Paper No. STD/DOC(2005)3).

OECD. (2008). *Handbook on constructing composite indicators: Methodology and user guide*. OECD Publishing. https://doi.org/10.1787/9789264043466-en

Ostrom, E. (1990). *Governing the commons: The evolution of institutions for collective action*. Cambridge University Press.

Postill, J., & Pink, S. (2012). Social media ethnography: The digital researcher in a messy web. *Media International Australia, 145*(1), 123–134. https://doi.org/10.1177/1329878X1214500114

Power, M. (1997). *The audit society: Rituals of verification*. Oxford University Press.

Reijers, W., Wright, A., & De Filippi, P. (2018). Blockchain governance and social contract theories. *Ledger, 3*, 134–151.

Scott, W. R. (2008). *Institutions and organizations: Ideas and interests* (3rd ed.). Sage Publications.

Tally.xyz. (2025). DAO governance dashboard. https://www.tally.xyz/

Taleb, N. N. (2012). *Antifragile: Things that gain from disorder*. Random House

Vergne, J.-P. (2021). Decentralized governance and the problem of opacity. *Journal of Organization Design, 10*, 1–18.

World Economic Forum. (2021). *Decentralized autonomous organizations: Beyond the hype* (White Paper). WEF Blockchain Consortium.

Wright, A., & De Filippi, P. (2015). *Decentralized blockchain technology and the rise of lex cryptographia* (SSRN Working Paper). https://ssrn.com/abstract=2580664

CHAPTER 4

Beyond the Code: Cultural and Behavioral Dynamics in DAOs

4.1 Introduction

While previous chapters addressed governance through diagnostic and structural lenses, this chapter focuses on the cultural substrate and behavioral dynamics that influence, enable, or distort those same structures.

Decentralized autonomous organizations (DAOs) are often described through the lens of code, smart contracts, and governance tokens. Yet governance is never purely technical: it is deeply shaped by cultural, psychological, and social dynamics that extend far beyond blockchain protocols. The code may define the rules, but it is human behavior that determines how those rules are interpreted, negotiated, or even subverted in practice.

While much of the literature on DAOs has focused on legal compliance, tokenomics, or protocol engineering, this chapter aims to shift the perspective to the "social layer" underlying decentralized governance. It positions itself at the intersection of political science, organizational theory, and behavioral economics, including Elinor Ostrom's design principles for commons governance, and concepts such as loss aversion, signaling, and bounded rationality, to argue that DAOs are as much social institutions as they are technological constructs. Understanding DAOs requires engaging not only with lines of code, but also with the rituals, narratives, and belief systems that sustain them as living communities.

A. Cesaretti, *DAO Governance in Theory and Practice*,
https://doi.org/10.1007/978-3-032-09675-3_4

At stake is a crucial insight: the sustainability and legitimacy of a DAO cannot be fully grasped without analyzing its invisible infrastructures of meaning, identity, and collective behavior. Power in DAOs does not flow solely from token balances or voting weights; it also arises from social influence, symbolic leadership, informal norms, and the subtle dynamics through which communities generate trust and legitimacy.

In exploring these dimensions, this chapter advocates for an ethnographic and behavioral approach to studying DAOs. Beyond quantitative metrics or protocol analysis, it argues that understanding decentralized communities requires observing everyday interactions, shared symbols, informal conversations, and cultural rituals. Ethnographic methods can reveal how meaning is constructed, how trust emerges, and how governance processes are experienced and contested from within—insights often invisible in purely technical or legal analyses.

This chapter therefore, seeks to answer questions such as:

- How do cultural narratives and collective identities shape governance outcomes in DAOs?
- In what ways do cognitive biases and social heuristics influence voting patterns and levels of participation?
- What role do rituals, symbols, and storytelling play in sustaining engagement and cohesion within decentralized communities?
- How can DAOs design governance architectures that account for the complexities and irrationalities of human psychology rather than assuming purely rational actors?

By unpacking these cultural and behavioral dynamics, we can begin to design DAOs that are not only secure and decentralized in code, but also resilient, inclusive, and adaptive as human communities. Ultimately, moving "beyond the code" is essential for building sustainable forms of decentralized governance that align technological possibilities with social realities.

4.2 DAOs as Socio-Technical Systems

4.2.1 Definition and Core Features of DAOs

Decentralized autonomous organizations (DAOs) are frequently defined as blockchain-based structures that operate without centralized leadership, governed instead by smart contracts and community-driven decision-making. Yet this technical description captures only part of the picture. DAOs are also social organisms, composed of people who share visions, values, and rituals, and who interact within complex webs of trust, reputation, and informal norms.

At a minimum, a DAO typically features:

- Smart contracts that encode operational rules, automate processes, and execute collective decisions.
- Governance tokens that enable participation in voting, proposal-making, and sometimes economic rights.
- On-chain voting mechanisms that record decisions transparently and, in principle, immutably.
- Treasury systems that manage shared resources, often with rules tied directly to governance decisions.

These components provide the technical skeleton of a DAO. But around this skeleton grows a flesh of human behavior, shared narratives, and social practices that fundamentally shape how a DAO functions in practice.

4.2.2 Interaction Between Technical Components and Social Dynamics

While DAOs are grounded in code, they are animated by culture. The technical layer, smart contracts, tokenomics, and voting mechanisms, define the possibility space of governance, but the social layer determines how that space is inhabited.

Several critical interactions illustrate this socio-technical entanglement:

- Smart contracts and informal trust: Even when rules are encoded in smart contracts, participants rely on off-chain discussions, community reputation, and informal agreements. Technical immutability does not erase the need for human negotiation and trust-building.
- Tokenomics and social signaling: Token distribution affects power structures but also serves as a signaling mechanism. Large token holders ("whales") can exert outsized influence not only through voting power but by shaping community perceptions, legitimizing projects, or discouraging dissent.

- Voting systems and participation culture: The existence of voting tools does not guarantee engagement. Cultural factors, such as community rituals, shared identity, and narrative cohesion, influence whether members actually show up to vote or delegate their power.
- Technical affordances and emergent behavior: Features like delegation, quadratic voting, or reputation-based weightings often produce unintended social consequences, from echo chambers to gatekeeping by elite groups.

In essence, DAOs operate as hybrid spaces where technical infrastructure and human culture continuously co-produce governance outcomes. Ignoring either dimension risks misunderstanding how decentralized governance truly works.

4.2.3 DAOs as Complex Adaptive and Self-Organizing Systems

Viewed through the lens of complexity theory, DAOs can be understood as complex adaptive systems. They consist of numerous interacting agents whose collective behavior gives rise to patterns and structures that are not centrally planned but emerge from local interactions.

Key characteristics of DAOs as complex systems include:

- Emergence: Collective decisions and cultural norms arise from countless individual actions, often producing outcomes that no single participant intended.
- Feedback loops: Positive and negative feedback mechanisms amplify or dampen behaviors. For example, successful proposals can attract new participants, while controversial votes may fracture communities.
- Adaptation: DAOs evolve in response to external shocks (regulatory changes, market volatility) and internal dynamics (conflicts, leadership shifts). They modify their governance structures, adjust quorum thresholds, or even fork into new entities.
- Non-linearity: Small actions can trigger disproportionate effects, especially in highly interconnected networks where sentiment and trust can change rapidly.
- Self-organization: Despite lacking a central authority, DAOs develop governance norms, specialized roles, and informal hierarchies through decentralized coordination.

Understanding DAOs as complex adaptive systems highlights why purely technical solutions to governance challenges often fall short. Governance mechanisms do not operate in a vacuum; they interact with psychological biases, cultural narratives, and evolving community dynamics. Designing sustainable DAOs thus requires embracing the unpredictability, flexibility, and emergent properties inherent to complex social systems.

DAOs can be seen as complex adaptive systems where rules emerge through local interactions and collective negotiation. As Ostrom (1990) demonstrated in her work on commons governance, sustainable institutions often rely on principles such as clearly defined boundaries, collective-choice arrangements, and mechanisms for monitoring and graduated sanctions. These principles are highly relevant for DAOs, which must balance code-based rules with social cooperation to avoid governance failures or free-riding.

4.3 Emerging Cultural Dynamics

4.3.1 Formation of Collective Identities and Sense of Belonging in DAOs

DAOs are not merely technical infrastructures; they are cultural and symbolic spaces in which participants construct shared identities, narratives, and forms of belonging. Drawing from the sociology of organizations and political anthropology, collective identity within DAOs can be understood as a dynamic process through which individuals align themselves with a community through symbolic, emotional, and ideological affiliations (Castells, 1997; Polletta & Jasper, 2001).

The formation of collective identity in DAOs is often catalyzed by three interrelated mechanisms:

- Narrative construction: Founding myths, slogans, and ideological statements, such as “exit to community,” “code is law,” or “decentralization by default,” serve not only as rhetorical tools but as performative acts of community-building. These narratives position the DAO within a broader political or economic mission, offering members a sense of purpose beyond instrumental participation (Snow & Benford, 1988; Nabben, 2021).

- Shared milestones and adversity: Community resilience is often forged through the experience of key events, including forks, governance crises, or collective wins (e.g., successful proposal campaigns). These episodes create symbolic memory and contribute to the internal cohesion of the group, functioning similarly to what Durkheim (1912) called "collective effervescence."
- Symbols of affiliation: The use of NFTs as identity markers, customized Discord roles, pseudonymous avatars, and governance badges contributes to the semiotic infrastructure of DAOs. These elements serve as visual and reputational tokens of membership, reinforcing the boundaries between insiders and outsiders (Turner, 1969; Goffman, 1959).

Collective identity in DAOs serves both integrative and normative functions: it sustains participation, fosters trust, and helps coordinate expectations. However, it also entails risks. Strong identity markers can lead to tribalism, reinforce in-group biases, or marginalize dissenting voices, especially when critique is conflated with disloyalty (Sunstein, 2009).

Thus, identity formation in DAOs is not a peripheral phenomenon, but a central driver of governance behavior. It shapes who participates, how legitimacy is constructed, and how decisions are interpreted and internalized by the community. As Ostrom (1990) noted in the study of commons, shared identity and mutual understanding are prerequisites for sustainable self-governance. In the context of DAOs, this suggests that designing governance mechanisms without attention to identity dynamics may result in technically sound but socially fragile institutions.

4.3.2 *Rituals, Language, and Shared Symbols Within DAO Communities*

Beyond technical architecture and formal governance structures, DAOs rely heavily on cultural mechanisms that generate social cohesion, shared meaning, and informal legitimacy. Rituals, symbolic language, and community-specific semiotics function as essential tools for both bonding and boundary-setting. These elements constitute what anthropologists and sociologists have long recognized as the "symbolic order" of institutions (Douglas, 1986; Geertz, 1973).

4.3.2.1 Ritual Practices

In DAO communities, rituals often take the form of recurring activities that reinforce collective identity and group norms. These include "Temperature checks" prior to formal votes, Weekly community calls or governance AMAs, Emoji reactions as meta-communication during debates, Periodic events like grant rounds or airdrop distributions. Such repetitive actions foster a sense of rhythm, familiarity, and participation, even in asynchronous or pseudonymous environments. As Turner (1969) observed in liminal social settings, rituals act as stabilizing mechanisms that help communities process ambiguity and maintain symbolic continuity.

4.3.2.2 Specialized Language and Jargon

DAOs often develop a distinctive lexicon, terms like rage quit, snapshot, governance mining, or WAGMI, that facilitates rapid internal communication but also functions as a gatekeeping device. Mastery of this language signals familiarity and status within the group, creating an "insider" culture that can foster both engagement and exclusion (Bourdieu, 1986; Goffman, 1959).

The performative use of such language not only streamlines communication but reinforces the cognitive frame through which governance processes are interpreted. Much like in subcultural groups, linguistic markers within DAOs shape how legitimacy, dissent, or innovation are perceived and discussed (Hebdige, 1979).

4.3.2.3 Memes, Symbols, and Visual Codes

DAOs are also steeped in symbolic imagery. Logos, avatars, and especially memes serve as powerful carriers of meaning. Memes, in particular, act as compressed narratives, enabling complex cultural signals to be transmitted with minimal friction (Shifman, 2014). In decentralized settings where formal branding is often absent or contested, memes help articulate group values, signal ideological alignment, and emotionally reinforce shared experiences.

Moreover, NFTs often operate as symbolic badges of belonging, blending cultural capital with economic participation. Their ownership and public display serve both as expressions of identity and as status markers, mirroring dynamics observed in prestige economies (Arvidsson & Peitersen, 2013).

Taken together, these symbolic elements form a ritual infrastructure that undergirds the governance mechanics of DAOs. While they are not part of the codebase, they shape who participates, how norms are enforced, and what counts as legitimate discourse. Ignoring these cultural dynamics risks underestimating the informal institutions that make DAOs function not just as technical systems, but as communities of meaning.

4.3.3 *Processes of Trust-Building and Social Legitimacy*

Trust and legitimacy are foundational pillars for any governance system, but in DAOs, where anonymity, decentralization, and code-based interactions prevail, it must be cultivated through alternative and often informal mechanisms. While blockchain infrastructure offers cryptographic guarantees, these are insufficient to sustain long-term cooperation without complementary layers of social trust and perceived fairness (Luhmann, 1979; Ostrom, 1990).

4.3.3.1 Reputation Systems as Social Infrastructure

Many DAOs implement either implicit or explicit reputation systems, tools that quantify and visualize user contributions, voting patterns, forum engagement, or project leadership. These systems serve as trust proxies, enabling community members to assess one another's reliability and alignment with shared values. As Friedman and Resnick (2001) argue, in distributed digital environments, well-designed reputation mechanisms can partially substitute for the institutional enforcement traditionally exercised by centralized actors.

However, these systems also risk entrenching elite dynamics, where early or well-connected participants accumulate disproportionate symbolic capital, which can in turn reproduce informal hierarchies (Piketty, 2014; Bourdieu, 1986).

4.3.3.2 Social Signaling and Endorsement Dynamics

In addition to quantifiable reputation, trust in DAOs is shaped by social signaling—who supports a proposal, which delegates endorse it, and what figures hold symbolic authority. This reflects the power of "soft legitimacy," whereby perceived alignment with community ethos influences voting behavior more than technical merit (Cialdini, 2001).

Signaling can also serve as a shortcut for epistemic trust, especially in complex environments where full rational analysis is infeasible. However, this dynamic may encourage herding behavior and reduce epistemic diversity (Sunstein, 2009).

4.3.3.3 Narrative-Based Legitimacy and Symbolic Decentralization

DAO legitimacy is often constructed through rhetorical commitments to decentralization, transparency, and community-driven decision-making. Project documentation, governance forums, and public statements frequently invoke ideals of openness and collective ownership, even in cases where decision-making power remains concentrated (Schneider, 2022).

This tension between symbolic decentralization and substantive control has been widely noted in the literature on Web3 governance (Choudhury & Koens, 2023; Hassan & Reijers, 2021). Legitimacy thus hinges not solely on technical affordances, but on the narratives communities use to frame their governance, and the consistency between those narratives and observed behavior.

4.3.3.4 Off-Chain Negotiation and Informal Governance

Despite the prominence of on-chain voting, much of DAO governance occurs in off-chain environments: Discord servers, private chats, governance calls, and Twitter debates. These informal spaces are where alliances are formed, consensus is built, and opposition is negotiated before reaching formal proposal stages.

Such informal governance parallels what Scott (1990) termed the "hidden transcript," the unofficial discourses and practices that coexist alongside formal procedures. Recognizing the role of these off-chain interactions is crucial for understanding how actual decision-making authority is exercised in DAOs.

In sum, trust and legitimacy in DAOs emerge not from code alone, but from complex social ecosystems where reputation, signaling, narrative coherence, and informal negotiation co-produce governance outcomes. Designing robust DAO governance therefore requires a dual focus: ensuring the transparency and integrity of formal processes, while fostering the relational and symbolic infrastructures that sustain legitimacy over time.

4.4 Individual and Collective Behaviors

Understanding the functioning of DAOs requires an analysis not only of institutional structures but also of the behavioral logics that shape participation and decision-making. Participants in decentralized communities are not purely rational agents acting in a vacuum of incentives; they are embedded in social environments, motivated by a complex interplay of economic interest, social recognition, and ideological alignment (March & Olsen, 1989; Ostrom, 1990). This section explores the motivational dynamics, cognitive limitations, and coordination strategies that influence DAO governance in the absence of centralized authority.

4.4.1 *Motivations for Participation: Altruism, Reputation, and Economic Incentives*

DAO participants are driven by a heterogeneous set of motivations, often coexisting and evolving over time:

- Economic incentives: Participation is frequently spurred by the expectation of financial rewards, including token distributions, airdrops, staking yields, or access to revenue-sharing mechanisms. However, as Deci & Ryan (1985) show, extrinsic incentives can sometimes crowd out intrinsic motivation, leading to short-termism or opportunistic behavior.
- Reputation and social capital: Many individuals contribute to DAOs in order to build reputation within the community, measured via public visibility, forum contributions, or leadership in working groups. This form of symbolic capital (Bourdieu, 1986) often translates into greater influence over governance outcomes, particularly in systems with delegate-based voting.
- Altruism and ideological commitment: A significant portion of DAO contributors are motivated by normative goals, such as promoting financial inclusion, supporting open-source development, or advancing decentralization as a political principle. These motivations are akin to what Hirschman (1982) called "voice" in public goods contexts, where engagement reflects commitment to shared ideals rather than instrumental gains.

Balancing these motivational layers is critical. Over-reliance on economic incentives can undermine community cohesion, while neglecting financial sustainability may lead to contributor burnout or attrition (Buterin, 2014).

4.4.2 *Cognitive Biases, Echo Chambers, and Polarization*

Despite their decentralized ideals, DAOs are not immune to cognitive biases and social dynamics that undermine deliberative quality:

- Loss aversion (Kahneman & Tversky, 1979): Participants may resist changes that entail potential downside risks, even if long-term gains are plausible. This can lead to inertia, conservatism in protocol upgrades, or rejection of experimental governance mechanisms.
- Social proof and herding: Visible endorsements by prominent delegates or developers can create bandwagon effects, skewing votes not by merit but by perceived consensus (Cialdini, 2001). This dynamic is amplified in fast-moving environments where decisions are time-sensitive.
- Confirmation bias: Users often gravitate toward information that supports their pre-existing views, reducing the space for critical debate and increasing ideological rigidity. Combined with algorithmic feed curation, this leads to epistemic silos and diminished diversity of opinion (Sunstein, 2009).
- Echo chambers and polarization: Online governance forums (e.g., Discord, Discourse) facilitate community bonding but can foster insularity, where dissent is subtly discouraged and opposition framed as disloyalty. Over time, this can result in factionalism, reducing institutional resilience.
- These vulnerabilities illustrate that rational choice models of governance are insufficient. Instead, DAOs must incorporate behaviorally-informed safeguards, such as deliberation phases, temperature checks, and diversity incentives, to mitigate polarization and enhance institutional learning.

4.4.3 Coordination and Decision-Making in the Absence of Traditional Hierarchies

DAOs are designed to operate without centralized control, but coordination without hierarchy remains a persistent challenge (Jensen & Meckling, 1976; Ostrom, 1990). Several mechanisms have emerged to address this tension:

- On-chain voting: Smart contract–based decision-making ensures transparency and immutability, but often suffers from low participation rates and token plutocracy.
- Delegation and liquid democracy: Allowing members to assign voting power to trusted representatives aims to balance efficiency with

representativeness. Yet, concentration of influence among "super-delegates" remains a critical risk (Choudhury & Koens, 2023).

- Informal leadership and soft power: In the absence of formal roles, reputational influence, social capital, and technical expertise often substitute for hierarchical authority. These soft forms of leadership are crucial but require transparency to avoid hidden centralization (Scott, 1990).
- Working groups and modular governance: Many DAOs develop task-specific teams to manage complexity and domain expertise. While effective, these structures can reintroduce silos or quasi-bureaucratic dynamics if not well-integrated into the broader governance flow.
- Narrative alignment and symbolic coordination: Shared values and collective missions often play a vital role in aligning actions, especially in ambiguous or crisis situations. This mirrors what Geertz (1973) described as the semiotic dimension of institutions—where meaning-making sustains cohesion more than formal procedures.

In practice, DAO coordination reflects a hybrid model: part algorithmic, part narrative, and part reputational. Recognizing these interdependencies is essential for designing resilient and inclusive governance frameworks.

4.5 Research Methodology

4.5.1 Digital Ethnographic Approach: Participant Observation, Forum Analysis, and Voting Records

Analyzing the cultural and behavioral dynamics of DAOs requires methodological frameworks capable of capturing not only formal processes but also the informal, affective, and symbolic dimensions of community life. To this end, this chapter adopts a digital ethnographic approach, which draws on the traditions of participant observation and qualitative content analysis, adapted to the specificities of online, decentralized environments (Boellstorff et al., 2012; Pink et al., 2016).

This approach enables the researcher to engage directly with community discourse, rituals, and norms, generating insights that are often inaccessible through quantitative analysis alone.

Key components of the methodology include:

Participant Observation
The researcher actively takes part in DAO communities by joining governance calls, engaging in Discord and Telegram channels, and contributing to forum discussions. This immersive stance allows the identification of tacit norms, informal hierarchies, and emotional dynamics that shape governance processes (Hine, 2000). Such involvement also facilitates understanding of the affective atmospheres (Wetherell, 2012) that underpin community cohesion, legitimacy, and conflict.

Qualitative Content Analysis of Online Forums
Platforms such as Discourse, Snapshot, GitHub, and governance-specific forums provide rich corpora of asynchronous interaction. Systematic analysis of these texts allows researchers to trace the emergence of shared narratives, symbolic vocabularies, and recurrent governance dilemmas. Coding and categorization techniques can be applied to identify themes such as power, trust, dissent, or collective identity (Geertz, 1973; Spradley, 1979).

Interpretation of On-Chain Voting Records
Quantitative data from governance platforms, such as proposal submissions, vote outcomes, and delegation flows, are analyzed in conjunction with the surrounding social context. While these records offer transparency and precision, they often obscure the informal deliberations and symbolic gestures that precede or accompany formal decisions (Reijers et al., 2018). A cross-reading of on-chain data and off-chain interactions is therefore essential to reconstruct the full spectrum of governance activity.

Unlike survey-based methods that elicit responses through predefined questions, digital ethnography provides access to naturally occurring interactions, enabling the researcher to observe how meaning, influence, and legitimacy are constructed in situ. It reveals how decentralized governance unfolds not just through code and votes, but through memes, emojis, informal discussions, and acts of narrative framing, what Scott (1990) would call the "hidden transcripts" of power.

This methodological stance aligns with the broader argument of the chapter: that DAOs must be understood as socio-technical systems, where formal structures interact with deeply human processes of identity, perception, and ritualized behavior.

4.5.2 Network Analysis Tools for Mapping Social Interactions

While ethnographic approaches offer valuable insight into the symbolic and experiential dimensions of DAO governance, network analysis provides a complementary lens for understanding how influence, information, and trust circulate within decentralized communities. DAOs are, by design, networked entities, not only at the technical level of blockchain architecture, but also at the social level of participant interactions, discourse flows, and informal coordination (Barabási, 2016; Newman, 2010).

Social network analysis (SNA) enables the mapping and measurement of these relational structures, offering empirical data on the distribution of attention, authority, and communicative centrality across DAO ecosystems.

Key Applications of Network Analysis in DAO Contexts

- Identifying Influential Actors and Hubs

By visualizing interactions such as forum mentions, message replies, endorsement patterns, and delegation flows, it becomes possible to identify individuals who function as connective hubs or authority nodes (Freeman, 1978). These actors often serve as gatekeepers, amplifiers, or bottlenecks within governance processes—even in systems nominally structured to avoid centralization.

- Analyzing Sub-Communities and Clusters

DAOs frequently develop internal subdivisions: working groups, thematic collectives, or ideological factions. SNA allows for the identification of modular structures or echo chambers (Sunstein, 2009), revealing the degree of internal cohesion or fragmentation. Network modularity measures and cluster detection algorithms can highlight when communities are becoming over-insulated, reducing the diversity of viewpoints in governance debates.

- Measuring Centralization vs. Decentralization

Key metrics such as degree centrality, betweenness centrality, and closeness centrality provide quantifiable indicators of how decision-making power and information are distributed (Wasserman & Faust, 1994). These indicators can be used to assess whether a DAO's actual governance patterns reflect its ideological commitments to decentralization.

- Tracing the Propagation of Cultural Artifacts

By analyzing the diffusion of memes, hashtags, emoji reactions, or specific symbolic references, network analysis can track how cultural narratives and symbols spread across communities. This allows researchers to observe how shared meaning emerges and which actors play key roles in legitimizing or contesting those meanings (Tufekci, 2017).

When integrated with digital ethnographic methods, SNA helps illuminate the structural dimension of influence, who speaks, who listens, who connects, and who is excluded. Importantly, it allows DAO researchers and practitioners to move beyond assumptions of flatness or neutrality, replacing them with empirical representations of actual relational dynamics. These insights can inform both the design of governance mechanisms and the development of inclusive participation strategies.

Together, ethnographic immersion and network analytics form a multilayered methodological toolkit for examining DAO governance not only as protocol, but as a living web of meaning, behavior, and interdependence.

4.5.3 Case Selection Criteria and Data Collection Methods

To ensure analytical rigor and relevance, this chapter adopts a purposeful case selection strategy based on the heterogeneity of DAO structures, the richness of available data, and the theoretical value of each case in illustrating core socio-technical dynamics.

4.5.3.1 Case Selection Criteria

The selection of DAOs for cultural and behavioral analysis is guided by the following criteria.

4.5.3.2 Diversity of Organizational Models

Cases are chosen to represent a variety of DAO types, protocol DAOs, grant DAOs, infrastructure DAOs, and community DAOs, ensuring comparative insight across governance architectures (Hassan et al., 2021).

4.5.3.3 Availability of Data

Only DAOs with accessible, transparent, and retrievable data are included. This encompasses on-chain data (e.g., voting records, proposal histories), off-chain data (e.g., forum threads, Discord conversations), and contextual metadata (e.g., documentation, audits, retrospectives).

4.5.3.4 *High Levels of Community Engagement*

Selected DAOs demonstrate sustained activity in governance processes, enabling meaningful observation of participation dynamics, decision-making routines, and informal leadership.

4.5.3.5 *Relevance to Theoretical Constructs*

Cases are prioritized when they offer empirical depth to key constructs explored in this chapter, such as ritual practices, collective identity formation, reputation dynamics, or trust-building mechanisms.

4.5.3.6 *Visibility and Influence Within the Web3 Ecosystem*

Prominent DAOs are often trendsetters, influencing governance discourse across multiple projects. Analyzing such cases allows the identification of emergent norms and practices that shape the broader DAO landscape.

4.5.3.7 *Data Collection Methods*

A mixed-methods approach is employed to combine qualitative richness with quantitative precision. This triangulation is essential for capturing the complex interplay between formal protocol and informal social behavior.

4.5.3.8 *Ethnographic Fieldnotes*

The researcher engages in direct observation, attending governance calls, participating in chat groups, and contributing to discussion forums. Fieldnotes are used to document affective atmospheres, role dynamics, and unspoken norms (Pink et al., 2016).

4.5.3.9 *Content Analysis of Textual Data*

Forums (e.g., Discourse), chats (e.g., Discord, Telegram), and governance portals (e.g., Snapshot) are systematically analyzed through qualitative coding, identifying themes, narratives, symbolic language, and recurring tensions.

4.5.3.10 *On-Chain Data Extraction and Analysis*

Tools such as Dune Analytics, Tally, DeepDAO, and Snapshot are used to extract data on proposal frequency, voting turnout, delegate behavior, and token distribution, enabling the generation of participation metrics and governance KPIs.

4.5.3.11 Network Visualization
Social network analysis (SNA) is employed to map connections among community members, track influence flows, and visualize the centralization or fragmentation of governance discourse.

4.5.3.12 Memetic and Symbolic Analysis
Memes, emojis, and visual artifacts are analyzed not only as aesthetic elements but as carriers of meaning, group identity, and governance sentiment (Milner, 2016). These artifacts often function as condensed expressions of community values or dissent.

4.5.3.13 Reputation and Trust metrics
Where applicable, reputation systems are analyzed for their design, distribution patterns, and correlation with influence or proposal outcomes. These indicators serve as proxies for informal legitimacy and social capital (Lima et al., 2022).

This methodology seeks to bridge the technical and the cultural, producing a comprehensive view of DAO governance as a layered, dynamic, and co-constructed process. The combination of case diversity, ethnographic depth, and computational analysis enhances both interpretive validity and generalizability, offering robust foundations for theory-building and practical application in the field of decentralized governance.

4.6 Case Studies

4.6.1 Rationale for Case Selection and Analytical Focus

To translate theoretical insights into practical understanding, this chapter conducts an in-depth analysis of selected DAOs whose diverse structures, missions, and community dynamics exemplify the socio-technical complexity discussed so far. The chosen cases, Gitcoin, Optimism, and ENS, were selected based on:

- Their prominence and influence within the Web3 ecosystem.
- Availability of rich data (on-chain and off-chain) for analysis.
- Clear manifestations of cultural, behavioral, and governance dynamics.
- Variability in organizational models and community engagement practices.

Each case study focuses on how technical design interacts with cultural practices to shape participation, trust, and governance effectiveness.

This multiple-case approach follows established principles of comparative case study methodology (Yin, 2018), aiming to explore both common patterns and divergent dynamics.

4.6.2 Gitcoin: Collaboration Dynamics and Funding Distribution

Gitcoin is a DAO that originated as a platform for funding open-source projects, gradually evolving into a sophisticated governance ecosystem focused on public goods funding. Its model leverages mechanisms like quadratic funding, matching pools, and thematic grants to allocate resources in a decentralized yet coordinated way.

Key socio-cultural dynamics:

- Community identity and narrative: Gitcoin cultivates a strong narrative around supporting public goods and fostering an ecosystem of mutual aid. Members often identify not merely as funders or grantees but as participants in a broader mission to sustain digital infrastructure.
- Quadratic funding as social signaling: The quadratic funding model encourages widespread small contributions, amplifying the perceived importance of projects with broad community support. However, it also creates incentives for sybil attacks or strategic funding patterns, requiring social trust and technical safeguards.
- Rituals and community practices: Gitcoin organizes regular “Grants Rounds,” which function almost like seasonal festivals within the community. These events foster a sense of shared purpose and momentum, while public leaderboards and funding milestones provide symbolic recognition.
- Reputation and legitimacy: Contributors, grant recipients, and even voting participants build reputations based on their engagement and perceived alignment with Gitcoin’s mission. This reputation shapes influence in governance discussions and proposal success rates.

The Gitcoin case underscores how technical funding mechanisms intertwine with social norms, identity-building, and trust dynamics, shaping the effectiveness and perceived fairness of decentralized resource allocation.

4.6.3 Optimism: Governance Processes and Community Engagement

Optimism is a prominent Layer-2 scaling solution for Ethereum that has developed a complex governance model involving both token-based voting and community-driven processes. Optimism's governance architecture exemplifies attempts to balance decentralization with practical operational needs.

Key socio-cultural dynamics:

- Dual-house governance: Optimism operates under a two-house system, the Token House and the Citizens' House. The former uses token-based voting, while the latter integrates identity-based participation aimed at fostering broader community involvement. This hybrid model reflects an attempt to mitigate purely plutocratic outcomes.
- Narratives of collective progress: The Optimism community often frames its mission as part of an ideological drive toward a more scalable, user-friendly Ethereum ecosystem. The narrative of contributing to Ethereum's broader success strengthens identity and participation.
- Transparency vs. complexity: While governance processes are public and well-documented, the dual-house model and the intricacies of proposal workflows can pose barriers for newcomers. This tension between transparency and cognitive overload is a recurring theme in DAO governance.
- Emergence of informal leaders: Despite formal structures, certain individuals, such as protocol developers, prominent community advocates, or large token holders, exert significant informal influence over debates and voting outcomes. Their endorsements often shape the trajectory of proposals.

Optimism illustrates how hybrid governance models seek to balance efficiency, inclusivity, and legitimacy, while revealing how cultural narratives and social dynamics shape community engagement and governance outcomes.

4.6.4 ENS: Digital Identity Management and User Participation

The Ethereum Name Service (ENS) DAO governs the protocol that provides human-readable names for Ethereum addresses (e.g., "alice.eth").

ENS plays a crucial role in shaping digital identity within the Ethereum ecosystem, making it both a technical infrastructure and a cultural symbol.

The ENS community reflects many of the governance challenges typical of digital knowledge commons (Frischmann, Madison & Strandburg, 2014), where symbolic ownership and identity play crucial roles alongside technical protocol design.

Key socio-cultural dynamics:

- Identity and belonging: Owning an ENS domain functions as both a practical tool and a symbol of identity and status within the Ethereum community. High-profile domains (e.g., vitalik.eth) carry significant social capital, influencing perceptions of legitimacy and reputation.
- Community rituals: Events like "ENS airdrops" and community voting on key proposals have become ritualistic moments that reinforce collective identity and reward engagement.
- Token-based governance challenges: Despite its commitment to decentralization, ENS governance has faced challenges related to token concentration, with large holders wielding outsized influence over decisions. This creates tension between ideals of decentralization and practical governance dynamics.
- Cultural symbolism: ENS names have become part of digital cultural expression, used in Twitter handles, Discord usernames, and NFT profiles, signaling belonging to Web3 culture and specific ideological communities.

ENS demonstrates how DAOs governing technical infrastructure can become cultural institutions, where digital identity, symbolic ownership, and governance intersect in complex ways.

4.7 Discussion of Findings

4.7.1 *Synthesis of Observed Cultural and Behavioral Dynamics*

The comparative analysis of Gitcoin, Optimism, and ENS confirms a core insight: DAOs cannot be understood as purely algorithmic structures. Rather, they operate as socio-technical ecosystems in which technical infrastructure, human behavior, and symbolic practices continuously co-produce governance outcomes. While each DAO presents its own architecture, mission, and cultural identity, the case studies reveal several recurrent dynamics that transcend specific organizational forms.

Technical architectures, smart contracts, voting mechanisms, reputation systems, are not neutral instruments but interact with cultural narratives, shared values, and symbolic rituals that shape their interpretation and use. As Geertz (1973) argued in his anthropological work, the meaning of structures emerges from the symbolic systems through which they are enacted.

Despite the rhetoric of decentralization, informal hierarchies often emerge within DAOs. Influence is frequently concentrated in the hands of high-reputation members, early token holders, or prominent communicators. These dynamics resonate with classic observations on the inevitability of elite formation in collective action (Michels, 1915), updated in the DAO context through token-based reputation and social signaling.

Engagement tends to spike around critical events, such as grant rounds, protocol upgrades, or governance crises, but often declines during periods of routine decision-making. This cyclical participation echoes patterns observed in other digital communities (Sunstein, 2009), where attention economies and emotional salience drive engagement more than procedural continuity.

Cultural artifacts, ranging from memes and NFTs to public rituals like snapshot votes or airdrops, play a crucial role in sustaining cohesion and transmitting group norms. These practices function not only as mechanisms of inclusion and identity-building, but also as instruments of legitimacy and social bonding (Turner, 1969; Leach, 1954). In this sense, DAOs are not merely governance platforms but symbolic communities.

These findings suggest that DAO governance cannot be fully captured through technical audits or tokenomics analysis alone. Cultural and behavioral dimensions, trust networks, informal leadership, symbolic capital, cognitive biases are equally essential to understanding how decisions are made, legitimated, and sustained. The DAO, in this light, appears not as a deterministic machine but as a living institution whose health depends on both code integrity and cultural vitality.

4.7.2 Cross-Case Comparison and Identification of Common Patterns

Although Gitcoin, Optimism, and ENS differ in mission, architecture, and community design, the comparative analysis reveals a constellation of recurring governance patterns that appear across decentralized ecosystems. These patterns highlight both the structural tensions and the adaptive capacities that shape the long-term viability of DAOs as institutional forms.

All three DAOs deploy narrative strategies to frame their identity and purpose, be it Gitcoin's commitment to public goods, Optimism's alignment with Ethereum's scalability, or ENS's role in digital identity infrastructure. These narratives are not merely rhetorical: they function as sources of normative alignment, shaping participant motivations and reinforcing legitimacy (Douglas, 1986; March & Olsen, 1989). In DAO settings, ideological coherence often substitutes for formal hierarchy, enabling coordination through shared meaning.

Despite formal equality of voting rights (or token rights), informal power asymmetries are visible in all three cases. High-reputation members, early adopters, and socially prominent contributors disproportionately influence discourse and decisions. These patterns reflect what Bourdieu (1986) termed symbolic capital: the accumulation of influence through recognition, rather than formal authority. In DAO ecosystems, visibility often translates into credibility, and credibility into informal power.

DAO governance mechanisms continually mediate the interaction between encoded rules and social behaviors. For instance, Optimism's dual-house system attempts to balance token-weighted decisions with community representation, while Gitcoin's quadratic funding model embeds normative values into its funding logic. Yet in all cases, technical designs generate unintended consequences, such as complexity barriers, plutocratic outcomes, or the formation of cliques, illustrating the challenge of governing complex adaptive systems (Holland, 1992).

All three DAOs exhibit signs of communication asymmetry and polarization. Participation tends to concentrate in high-salience forums, often leading to the marginalization of dissenting voices or minority viewpoints. As Cialdini (2001) and Sunstein (2009) have shown, group dynamics in ideologically homogeneous environments can foster conformity, groupthink, and reduced deliberative quality. In DAOs, this dynamic may be exacerbated by anonymity, real-time interactions, and the performative nature of discourse.

None of the DAOs examined relies purely on on-chain governance. Instead, they combine formal mechanisms with off-chain negotiation, informal deliberation, and narrative framing. Whether through Discord discussions, retrospective analyses, or symbolic rituals, these off-chain practices play a central role in decision-making and community alignment.

This hybrid model suggests that DAO governance is better conceptualized as a layered and iterative process, rather than a single voting event or contract execution.

These cross-case observations suggest that DAO governance is shaped as much by cultural infrastructure and behavioral dynamics as by code. Effective decentralization does not imply the absence of structure, but rather the emergence of new forms of order, mediated by narrative, ritual, and informal norms. Recognizing these common patterns is essential for both evaluative purposes and for guiding the design of future decentralized institutions that are not only robust in code, but also resilient in practice.

4.7.3 Implications for DAO Design and Management

The patterns identified across Gitcoin, Optimism, and ENS are not merely descriptive; they carry practical implications for those who design, manage, or participate in DAOs. As decentralized organizations mature, they must confront a central paradox: governance structures cannot be reduced to technical protocols alone, yet neither can they rely solely on cultural alignment or goodwill. Successful DAO design requires a hybrid approach that weaves together the affordances of code with the unpredictability of human behavior.

1. Design with social dynamics in mind

Many DAO failures stem from the naïve assumption that rational actors will engage with systems as intended, provided incentives are properly aligned. Yet, as shown by behavioral economics (Kahneman, 2011; Sunstein, 2009), participants often act based on bounded rationality, emotional heuristics, or social mimicry. DAO architects must therefore account for loss aversion, social signaling, and group polarization when designing participation flows, voting systems, or reward mechanisms.

2. Acknowledge and manage informal power

Informal leadership, symbolic authority, and reputation-driven influence are unavoidable in decentralized settings (Bourdieu, 1986; Scott, 1990). Rather than denying their existence, DAOs should develop mechanisms to monitor and balance these forces. Transparency dashboards, reputation audits, and rotating roles can help expose hidden hierarchies and prevent the ossification of power within informal elites.

3. Cultivate narrative and identity

Narratives are more than storytelling devices; they are coordination tools. Strong collective identities anchored in shared myths, symbols, and values enhance resilience, motivation, and coherence, particularly during periods of uncertainty or conflict (Geertz, 1973; March & Olsen, 1989). DAOs should intentionally foster cultural cohesion through rituals, shared milestones, and inclusive language that welcomes newcomers while reinforcing shared purpose.

4. Design for accessibility and cognitive diversity

Excessive technical complexity discourages participation, concentrates power among specialists, and widens the gap between core contributors and the broader community. Governance tools should therefore aim for cognitive accessibility, clear interfaces, tiered participation, and explanatory resources. Moreover, systems should protect and amplify minority perspectives, enabling genuine deliberation rather than algorithmic consensus.

5. Embed adaptability into governance

Rigid systems are brittle. DAOs should embrace their nature as living, evolving institutions by incorporating structured feedback loops, retrospective analysis, and pathways for constitutional reform. Just as biological systems survive through mutation and selection, DAOs thrive when they can experiment, learn, and iterate (Holland, 1992; Ostrom, 1990).

6. Balance automation with human judgment

While code enables transparency, predictability, and trustless execution, some decisions require discretion, empathy, or ethical reflection. DAOs should define clear domains where human deliberation complements algorithmic processes, especially in areas such as dispute resolution, emergency governance, or value-sensitive design.

In conclusion, these implications reinforce a central insight of this chapter: DAO governance is not only a technical challenge, but a cultural and psychological one. The path toward robust decentralization lies in recognizing that institutions are sustained by more than code. They are built through meaning, trust, and collective care

4.7.4 *Limitations and Directions for Future Research*

This chapter has outlined a socio-cultural framework for understanding DAOs, integrating ethnographic insights with network analysis and behavioral theory. While this approach provides a richer, multi-dimensional perspective, it also entails several limitations and opens space for further investigation.

1. Methodological Constraints

Digital ethnography, while effective in capturing informal dynamics, is subject to researcher bias, selective visibility, and the challenge of distinguishing signal from noise in noisy online spaces. Anonymity and pseudonymity complicate efforts to establish clear chains of influence or accountability (Giddens, 1984).

2. Limited Generalizability

The case studies of Gitcoin, Optimism, and ENS offer depth, but represent a narrow segment of the DAO ecosystem, primarily high-profile, Ethereum-based, and relatively well-resourced. Their cultural dynamics may differ from those of smaller DAOs, non-financial collectives, or organizations on alternative chains.

3. Data Availability Bias

Most research was conducted on DAOs with publicly accessible governance data and active community forums. Many DAOs, particularly early-stage or closed-ecosystem ones, operate without such transparency, limiting analytical reach and possibly underestimating informal or opaque governance models.

4. Need for Longitudinal Data

Understanding cultural shifts, trust erosion, or participation fatigue requires long-term observation, especially across multiple governance cycles, crises, or forks. Current snapshots cannot fully capture the temporal dimension of DAO evolution or the compounding effects of cultural practices over time (Geertz, 1973; Holland, 1992).

Future Research Directions

To address these limitations and deepen the analytical toolkit, future research should explore:

- Longitudinal ethnographic studies tracking community culture across governance reforms, crises, or forks.
- Cross-platform comparison of DAOs beyond Ethereum, including Cosmos, Solana, or Polkadot-based structures.
- Comparative typologies between social DAOs, protocol DAOs, grant-giving DAOs, and network states, to uncover archetypes of cultural dynamics.
- Quantitative analysis of sentiment vs. voting patterns, linking on-chain behavior with off-chain discourse.
- Experimental methods, such as controlled governance simulations, to test the impact of narratives, identity signals, or trust markers on governance outcomes.
- Hybrid methodological frameworks, combining digital ethnography, social network analysis, and automated text analysis to track symbolic patterns, participation decay, or the spread of disinformation.

As illustrated in Fig. 4.1, DAO governance is shaped by the interplay of four interdependent dimensions:

- Culture: Narratives, rituals, and symbolic systems that establish belonging and meaning.
- Behavior: Motivations, cognitive biases, and decision-making patterns of individuals.
- Relationships: Trust networks, reputation signals, and social legitimacy mechanisms.
- Structure: Coordination tools, working groups, delegation systems, and informal leadership.

These dynamics do not operate in isolation; they interact to form a complex and adaptive ecosystem. Future research must continue to map and understand this ecosystem if DAOs are to evolve into sustainable, inclusive, and effective governance systems.

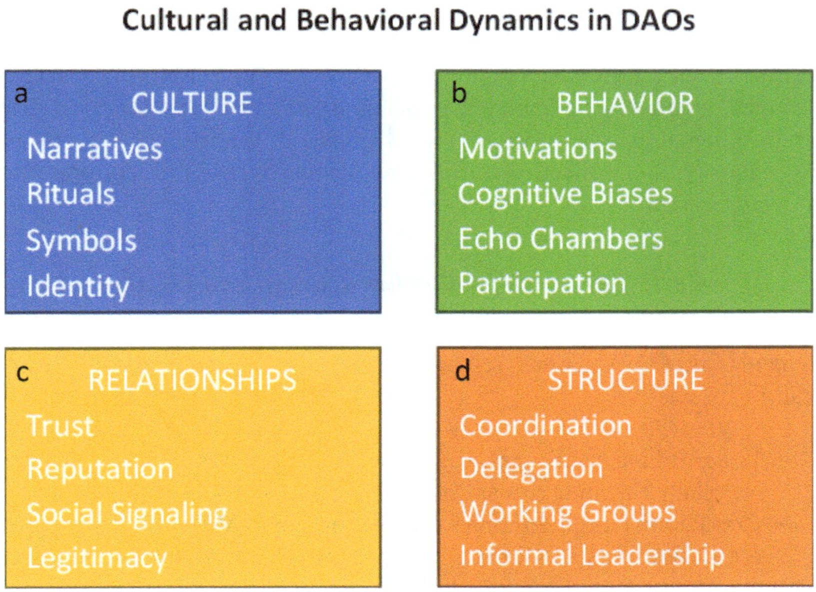

Fig. 4.1 Four dimensions of cultural and behavioral dynamics in DAOs. This infographic summarizes the key dimensions that shape DAO governance beyond formal code and protocols. **a**. Culture encompasses narratives, rituals, and shared symbols that sustain identity and belonging. **b**. Behavior refers to individual motivations, cognitive biases, and participation dynamics that influence decision-making. **c**. Relationships highlight trust networks, reputation systems, and mechanisms of social legitimacy. **d**. Structure refers to coordination tools, delegation practices, and emergent forms of leadership and organization. Together, these layers interact to form the invisible architecture of DAO communities, with profound implications for legitimacy, sustainability, and governance effectiveness

4.8 Conclusions and Future Perspectives

4.8.1 Reflections on the Importance of Cultural Dimensions in DAOs

This chapter has argued that DAOs cannot be fully understood, or successfully designed, by focusing solely on code, tokenomics, or legal frameworks. They are socio-technical systems where algorithms and protocols interact with human behavior, cultural narratives, and social rituals.

Cultural dynamics shape how governance structures are perceived, how decisions are made, and how trust is built and sustained.

Recognizing DAOs as cultural ecosystems does not diminish the role of technical architecture; rather, it enriches it. Effective decentralized governance demands an appreciation for the invisible infrastructures of meaning, identity, and collective norms that determine whether communities thrive or fracture.

4.8.2 *Proposals for Further Research and Inquiry*

While this chapter provides an initial exploration of cultural and behavioral dynamics in DAOs, much remains to be investigated. Future research could explore:

- Longitudinal studies tracking how DAO cultures evolve over time, especially through crises, leadership changes, or regulatory shifts.
- Comparative ethnographies across different DAO types (e.g., protocol DAOs vs. social DAOs) to identify unique and shared cultural features.
- Quantitative studies linking network analysis metrics to cultural indicators, such as sentiment, trust levels, or participation volatility.
- Interdisciplinary frameworks integrating insights from anthropology, political science, behavioral economics, and network theory to produce more comprehensive models of DAO governance.

Such inquiries would not only deepen academic understanding but also generate practical insights for DAO designers and community leaders.

4.8.3 *Suggestions for Practitioners and DAO Designers*

For practitioners and DAO architects, several practical lessons emerge from this exploration:

- Design for culture, not just code: Governance mechanisms should explicitly account for social behaviors, cognitive biases, and symbolic practices that influence participation and legitimacy.
- Foster narrative and identity: Strong narratives and shared identities help sustain engagement and resilience, particularly during periods of uncertainty or conflict.

- Monitor informal power structures: Even decentralized systems produce informal hierarchies. Understanding and managing these dynamics is crucial for maintaining transparency and inclusivity.
- Balance simplicity and nuance: Governance tools must be accessible enough to encourage participation yet nuanced enough to handle the complexities of human behavior and community dynamics.
- Embrace adaptability: DAO governance should be conceived as an iterative process, open to revision as communities grow, learn, and evolve.

Ultimately, the promise of DAOs lies not merely in technological innovation but in building new forms of human collaboration. To fulfill that promise, practitioners must engage not only with protocols and tokens but with the deeper cultural currents that animate decentralized communities.

These insights lay the foundation for the next chapter, which addresses the design implications of complexity and uncertainty in DAO governance.

4.9 Design Takeaways: Cultural and Behavioral Dynamics in DAO Governance

1. Culture shapes code interpretation

Governance is not neutral: rituals, narratives, and identity influence how rules are enacted, contested, or bypassed.

2. Informal power matters

Even in decentralized systems, social capital, reputation, and narrative control produce emergent hierarchies and gatekeeping dynamics.

3. Participation is psychological, not just procedural

Voting tools alone do not ensure engagement—motivation, cognitive load, and perceived legitimacy deeply affects governance activity.

4. Trust is social as well as cryptographic

Reputation systems, signaling, and shared norms sustain cohesion, but can also obscure centralized influence under the guise of "community-driven" processes.

5. Design for complexity and ambiguity

DAOs are complex adaptive systems. Robust governance emerges from embracing emergent behavior, feedback loops, and socio-technical hybridity.

References

Arvidsson, A., & Peitersen, N. (2013). *The ethical economy: Rebuilding value after the crisis*. Columbia University Press.

Barabási, A. L. (2016). *Network science*. Cambridge University Press.

Boellstorff, T., Nardi, B., Pearce, C., & Taylor, T. L. (2012). *Ethnography and virtual worlds: A handbook of method*. Princeton University Press.

Bourdieu, P. (1986). The forms of capital. In J. Richardson (Ed.), *Handbook of theory and research for the sociology of education*. Greenwood.

Buterin, V. (2014). *DAOs, DACs, DAs and more: An incomplete terminology guide*. Ethereum Foundation Blog. https://ethereum.org/en/blog/2014/05/06/daos-dacs-das-and-more/

Castells, M. (1997). *The power of identity*. Blackwell Publishers.

Choudhury, N., & Koens, K. (2023). *Measuring DAO maturity: Frameworks for reflexive governance* (DAO Research Collective Working Paper Series).

Cialdini, R. B. (2001). *Influence: Science and practice* (4th ed.). Allyn & Bacon.

Deci, E. L., & Ryan, R. M. (1985). *Intrinsic motivation and self-determination in human behavior*. Springer.

Douglas, M. (1986). *How institutions think*. Syracuse University Press.

Durkheim, É. (1912). Les Formes Élémentaires de la Vie Religieuse. Paris: Alcan. (English trans. The elementary forms of religious life, Free Press, 1995).

Foucault, M. (1977). *Discipline and punish: The birth of the prison*. Pantheon Books.

Freeman, L. C. (1978). Centrality in social networks: Conceptual clarification. *Social Networks, 1*(3), 215–239.

Friedman, E., & Resnick, P. (2001). The social cost of cheap pseudonyms. *Journal of Economics & Management Strategy, 10*(2), 173–199.

Frischmann, B. M., Madison, M. J., & Strandburg, K. J. (2014). *Governing knowledge commons*. Oxford University Press.

Geertz, C. (1973). *The interpretation of cultures*. Basic Books.
Giddens, A. (1984). *The constitution of society: Outline of the theory of structuration*. University of California Press.
Goffman, E. (1959). *The presentation of self in everyday life*. Anchor Books.
Hassan, S., & Reijers, W. (2021). *Institutional design for DAO governance* (DAO Research Collective Working Paper Series).
Hassan, S., Reijers, W., & Wiertz, C. (2021). *Distributed governance and the commons* (DAO Research Collective Working Paper Series).
Hebdige, D. (1979). *Subculture: The meaning of style*. Routledge.
Hine, C. (2000). *Virtual ethnography*. Sage Publications.
Hirschman, A. O. (1982). *Shifting involvements: Private interest and public action*. Princeton University Press.
Holland, J. H. (1992). Complex adaptive systems. *Daedalus, 121*(1), 17–30.
Jensen, M. C., & Meckling, W. H. (1976). Theory of the firm: Managerial behavior, agency costs and ownership structure. *Journal of Financial Economics, 3*(4), 305–360.
Kahneman, D. (2011). *Thinking, fast and slow*. Farrar, Straus and Giroux.
Kahneman, D., & Tversky, A. (1979). Prospect theory: An analysis of decision under risk. *Econometrica, 47*(2), 263–292.
Leach, E. R. (1954). *Political systems of Highland Burma*. Harvard University Press.
Le Bon, G. (1895). *The crowd: A study of the popular mind*. T. Fisher Unwin.
Lima, I., Nabben, K., & Morselli, F. (2022). *DAO cultures and coordination patterns*. DAO Research Collective.
Luhmann, N. (1979). *Trust and power*. Wiley.
March, J. G., & Olsen, J. P. (1989). *Rediscovering institutions: The organizational basis of politics*. Free Press.
Michels, R. (1915). *Political parties: A sociological study of the oligarchical tendencies of modern democracy*. Free Press.
Milner, R. M. (2016). *The world made meme: Public conversations and participatory media*. MIT Press.
Nabben, K. (2021). *Decentralized autonomous organizations as governance experiments: Resilience, risks, and the future of democracy*. RMIT University Working Paper.
Newman, M. E. J. (2010). *Networks: An introduction*. Oxford University Press.
Ostrom, E. (1990). *Governing the commons: The evolution of institutions for collective action*. Cambridge University Press.
Piketty, T. (2014). *Capital in the twenty-first century*. Harvard University Press.
Pink, S., Horst, H., Postill, J., Hjorth, L., Lewis, T., & Tacchi, J. (2016). *Digital ethnography: Principles and practice*. Sage Publications.
Polletta, F., & Jasper, J. M. (2001). Collective identity and social movements. *Annual Review of Sociology, 27*, 283–305.

Reijers, W., Wright, A., & De Filippi, P. (2018). Blockchain governance and social contract theories. *Ledger*, *3*, 134–151.

Schneider, N. (2022). *Governable spaces: Democratic design for online life*. University of California Press.

Scott, J. C. (1990). *Domination and the arts of resistance: Hidden transcripts*. Yale University Press.

Snow, D. A., & Benford, R. D. (1988). Ideology, frame resonance, and participant mobilization. *International Social Movement Research*, *1*, 197–217.

Spradley, J. P. (1979). *The ethnographic interview*. Holt, Rinehart & Winston.

Sunstein, C. R. (2009). *Going to extremes: How like minds unite and divide*. Oxford University Press.

Szabo, N. (1997). Formalizing and securing relationships on public networks. *First Monday*, *2*(9), https://doi.org/10.5210/fm.v2i9.548

Tufekci, Z. (2017). *Twitter and tear gas: The power and fragility of networked protest*. Yale University Press.

Turner, V. (1969). *The ritual process: Structure and anti-structure*. Aldine Publishing.

Wasserman, S., & Faust, K. (1994). *Social network analysis: Methods and applications*. Cambridge University Press.

Wetherell, M. (2012). *Affect and emotion: A new social science understanding*. Sage Publications.

Yin, R. K. (2018). *Case study research and applications: Design and methods* (6th ed.). Sage Publications.

CHAPTER 5

Network-Driven Valuation of Decentralized Organizations: Theoretical Models and Empirical Perspectives

5.1 Introduction

Building upon the limitations of traditional governance metrics outlined in Chap. 2 and the cultural dynamics explored in Chap. 4, this chapter presents a multidimensional framework for evaluating DAO value grounded in network theory and performance indicators.

Over the past decade, the rise of decentralized autonomous organizations (DAOs) has marked a significant transformation in the structure of digital economies.

DAOs represent a new paradigm of collective coordination, enabled by blockchain technology and smart contracts, promising more transparent, participatory, and resilient forms of governance compared to traditional centralized institutions.

Despite the growing adoption of DAOs across various sectors, from decentralized finance (DeFi) to social communities and investment vehicles, a fundamental challenge remains largely unresolved: how can the economic value of a DAO be properly measured?

Traditional valuation methods, such as those based solely on market capitalization, treasury size, or number of token holders, often fail to capture the real dynamics and sustainable potential of decentralized networks.

A. Cesaretti, *DAO Governance in Theory and Practice*,
https://doi.org/10.1007/978-3-032-09675-3_5

Moreover, metrics commonly used for corporate valuation do not fully translate into the decentralized, community-driven environment of DAOs, where participation, governance efficiency, and network effects play a crucial role.

This research aims to address this gap by proposing a set of new metrics for DAO valuation.

Building upon network theory principles, such as Metcalfe's Law, Reed's Law, and Beckstrom's Law, and integrating effective participation analysis, we seek to construct a more comprehensive, realistic framework for assessing the economic value of decentralized organizations.

Through a combination of theoretical modeling and empirical observation, this work aspires to contribute both to the academic understanding and to the practical evaluation of DAOs in the evolving digital economy.

This chapter presents original analysis based on publicly accessible governance data and qualitative observation of DAO ecosystems. The absence of bibliographic references is intentional: the interpretations and the DAO Health Index (DHI) framework are the result of independent research, not derived from prior academic literature. The chapter aims to illustrate how data-driven indicators can support a critical reading of DAO governance, without relying on existing theoretical models.

5.2 State of the Art

5.2.1 Why Valuing a DAO Matters

Decentralized autonomous organizations (DAOs) represent a new paradigm of collective coordination, operating without the traditional legal and organizational structures of corporations, cooperatives, or trusts. They are not legal entities in the conventional sense, but rather social constructs, sustained by blockchain-based smart contracts and community governance processes.

This non-entity nature raises a fundamental question:

- Why should we attempt to value a DAO at all?
- And if so, in what circumstances does such a valuation become relevant or meaningful?

The answer lies in understanding that, despite lacking formal legal personality, DAOs increasingly act as economic agents, managing treasuries, allocating capital, coordinating work, and exercising governance over digital and real-world resources.

Their ability to create, sustain, and distribute value makes them subject to many of the same evaluative pressures traditionally applied to companies, projects, or financial assets, albeit through different mechanisms.

5.2.2 *Strategic Contexts Where DAO Valuation is Relevant*

Valuing a DAO becomes crucial in several strategic contexts, especially when interpreted through the lens of decentralized finance and community governance models, which differ fundamentally from traditional corporate structures.

In each case, it is essential to identify who benefits from the valuation and through what medium the value is realized, recognizing that the instruments and beneficiaries often diverge from classical financial paradigms.

1. Investment Decision-Making

Beneficiaries: Investors, grant providers, strategic partners.

Medium: Ownership or governance rights expressed through tokens, reputational capital, or future claims over DAO-managed assets.

Unlike traditional equity investment, investors in a DAO typically acquire influence (voting power) and exposure to future upside through governance tokens or participation rights, not direct ownership of a legal entity's assets.

2. Mergers, Partnerships, and Treasury Integrations

Beneficiaries: Existing DAO members, merging DAOs, and new collective entities.

Medium: Access to combined treasuries, joint governance structures, and merged project portfolios.

Mergers in the DAO space involve the pooling of assets and governance capabilities, not the legal transfer of ownership. The value created benefits participants through shared decision-making power and expanded resource bases.

3. Token Pricing and Market Analysis

Beneficiaries: Token holders, investors, traders.

Medium: Price appreciation of governance tokens, enhanced liquidity, and improved market reputation.

Token valuation reflects market perception of the DAO's future performance and governance stability, similar to how stock prices reflect corporate fundamentals but without the backing of traditional legal claims.

4. Asset Liquidation and Sunset Processes

Beneficiaries: DAO members, treasury stakeholders.

Medium: Redistribution of treasury assets (e.g., stablecoins, tokens, NFTs) according to pre-defined governance rules.

In the absence of a legal framework for liquidation, DAOs execute dissolution through on-chain governance mechanisms, directly allocating digital assets to participants according to voting outcomes or contractual arrangements.

5. Risk Assessment and Governance Rating

Beneficiaries: Investors, insurance protocols, institutional partners.

Medium: Informed decision-making, insurance coverage, risk pricing.

Evaluating governance robustness and systemic resilience serves as a proxy for risk assessment, replacing traditional audits or legal due diligence with dynamic, on-chain behavioral analysis.

This approach reflects a fundamental paradigm shift: value in DAOs is not anchored in legal ownership but in participation rights, access to shared resources, and influence over collective decision-making. Understanding and measuring this form of decentralized value requires new frameworks and tools, distinct from those used in traditional corporate finance.

5.2.3 *The Nature of DAO Value: Beyond Financial Metrics*

Valuing a DAO does not simply mean estimating its treasury balance or token market cap. DAO value is inherently multi-dimensional, encompassing:

- Governance resilience: The ability of the DAO to maintain effective, inclusive, and sustainable decision-making processes over time.
- Community vitality: The quality and intensity of participation, innovation, and collaboration among members.
- Operational and economic efficiency: The DAO's ability to deploy resources effectively, minimize coordination costs, and generate tangible outputs (products, services, funded projects, community initiatives).
- Asset management capacity: Particularly in DeFi and NFT-oriented DAOs, the management and growth of digital assets become key elements of intrinsic value.

Thus, DAO valuation requires a broader lens that captures both structural robustness and dynamic performance over time.

5.2.4 The Need for a New Valuation Framework

Traditional valuation models, focused on static indicators like market capitalization, total value locked (TVL), or token holder counts, are insufficient to grasp the complex reality of DAOs.

The decentralized, participatory, and often rapidly evolving nature of DAOs demands a multi-dimensional, dynamic evaluation framework. Such a framework must integrate:

- network value effects (connectivity and collaboration potential),
- participation quality and governance metrics,
- economic output generation and sustainability indicators.

The following sections propose a new methodology that aims to bridge this gap, offering a comprehensive, flexible, and pragmatic tool for DAO valuation, adapted to the realities of decentralized economic and social coordination.

As illustrated in Fig. 5.1, the proposed framework evaluates DAO value through three interrelated dimensions: network value (CNVS), governance health (GHS), and economic output (EOS), each associated with a set of measurable KPIs.

DAO Valuation Framework - Dimensions and KPIs

Network Value (CNVS)

- Unique active wallets
- Governance token distribution
- Interaction density (on-chain & off-chain)

Governance Health (GHS)

- Participation rate
- Delegation ratio
- Proposal diversity
- Quorum effectiveness

Economic Output (EOS)

- Treasury growth
- Funded project success rate
- Revenue or value flow to stakeholders

Fig. 5.1 DAO valuation framework: Dimensions and KPIs. The composite framework assesses the value of decentralized organizations through three pillars: network activity and connectivity (CNVS), governance participation and quality (GHS), and measurable economic outcomes (EOS). Each dimension includes targeted KPIs derived from empirical DAO practices

5.2.5 *Traditional Metrics for DAO Valuation*

Despite the rapid expansion and growing influence of DAOs, the methods used to evaluate their economic value have remained relatively basic. The most common metrics include:

- Market capitalization: The total market value of a DAO's native token supply, calculated as the circulating supply multiplied by the current token price.
- Total value locked (TVL): The total amount of assets (in USD terms) locked within the DAO's smart contracts, particularly relevant for DeFi protocols.
- Number of token holders or members: The total count of individual wallets or users holding the governance token or participating in the DAO's activities.

While these indicators offer a surface-level snapshot of the DAO's size and apparent market traction, they often fail to capture deeper aspects of organizational health, governance quality, and sustainability.

5.2.6 *Limitations of Traditional Metrics*

Traditional valuation metrics present several critical limitations when applied to DAOs:

- Market capitalization is highly volatile and can be influenced by speculative trading, providing little insight into the intrinsic value or long-term viability of the organization.
- TVL can be misleading, especially in cases where liquidity incentives (such as yield farming rewards) artificially inflate the amount of locked assets without corresponding user engagement or protocol utility.
- The number of token holders does not necessarily reflect active participation, governance involvement, or the true strength of the community. Many DAOs face issues of voter apathy, with only a small fraction of holders actively participating in governance.

Moreover, these metrics tend to overlook key qualitative factors such as:

- The effectiveness of decision-making processes.
- The resilience of the community.
- The alignment of incentives among stakeholders.
- The ability to generate real-world economic outputs.

Thus, there is a pressing need for a new set of evaluation criteria that better reflects the unique dynamics and value-creation mechanisms of DAOs.

5.3 Network Theories Applied to DAO Valuation

The economic value of a DAO is inherently linked to the network structure that underpins it. Understanding how networks generate, amplify, and sustain value is therefore essential to designing meaningful valuation models for DAOs.

This chapter explores three key network theories, Metcalfe's Law, Reed's Law, and Beckstrom's Law, that provide foundational insights into the relationship between user participation, connection dynamics, and economic outcomes in decentralized systems.

Each theory highlights different mechanisms of value creation, offering complementary perspectives that will inform the development of a more comprehensive evaluation framework in the following chapters.

5.3.1 *Metcalfe's Law: The Quadratic Value of Connections*

Metcalfe's Law posits that the value of a network grows proportionally to the square of the number of its nodes (n^2).

Formulated by Robert Metcalfe in the 1980s, the law suggests that as more users join a network, the number of potential connections increases exponentially, enhancing the network's overall utility and value.

In the context of DAOs, Metcalfe's Law implies that the more members a DAO has, the more interactions, collaborations, and transactions become possible, theoretically increasing the organization's value.

However, Metcalfe's model assumes that all connections are equally valuable and that all users are equally active, which may not hold true in decentralized communities characterized by varying levels of participation.

5.3.2 *Reed's Law: The Exponential Value of Subgroups*

Reed's Law, introduced by David P. Reed in 1999, builds upon Metcalfe's insights but highlights the value generated not just by individual connections, but by the formation of groups and sub-communities.

According to Reed's Law, the utility of large networks, particularly social networks, can grow exponentially (2^n) with the number of users because of the countless potential group formations.

For DAOs, this perspective is highly relevant: the true value of a DAO may not lie merely in its size, but in its ability to foster working groups, task forces, specialized committees, and project-specific teams. Each subgroup can generate distinct forms of value, ideation, development, advocacy, that are not linearly dependent on the number of participants but exponentially amplified through collaboration.

5.3.3 Beckstrom's Law: Value as the Sum of Economic Savings

Beckstrom's Law, proposed by Rod Beckstrom in 2009, offers a different and more economically grounded perspective.

It asserts that the value of a network is equivalent to the sum of the savings generated for its users by their participation in the network, compared to the alternatives outside of it.

Applied to DAOs, Beckstrom's Law suggests that a DAO's value should be measured by the extent to which it reduces:

- Coordination costs.
- Transaction costs.
- Governance overhead.
- Trust-building expenses (through trustless smart contracts).

In this model, the economic efficiency achieved by decentralization and automation becomes the primary driver of value, rather than mere connectivity or community size.

The following graph illustrates the comparative growth patterns suggested by Metcalfe's Law, Reed's Law, and Beckstrom's Law.

It highlights the quadratic, exponential, and linear nature of value generation in networked structures.

5.3.4 Adaptations and Limitations: Applying Network Theories to DAOs

While Metcalfe's, Reed's, and Beckstrom's models provide valuable insights, applying them directly to DAOs requires careful adaptation:

- Unequal participation: Not all DAO members are equally active. Network value must be weighted by effective participation, not just presence.
- Quality over quantity: Connections or subgroups vary widely in quality, coherence, and productivity.
- Economic externalities: The savings generated by DAOs may not always be easily measurable, especially in early-stage or experimental organizations.

- Governance complexity: Decision-making mechanisms within DAOs (e.g., voting systems, delegation, reputation scores) introduce new dimensions that pure network theory does not fully address.

Therefore, while network theories offer a solid conceptual foundation, an effective valuation model for DAOs must integrate participation analysis, interaction quality, and economic output measures alongside traditional network growth functions.

While traditional network theories provide valuable insights into the potential value dynamics of decentralized organizations, they are not sufficient on their own to fully capture the unique characteristics of DAOs.

Effective valuation must go beyond theoretical network growth functions to incorporate factors such as participation quality, governance efficiency, economic sustainability, and real-world outcomes.

In light of these considerations, the next chapter proposes a new framework for evaluating the economic value of DAOs.

This framework combines adapted network models with original key performance indicators (KPIs) specifically designed to reflect the operational, participatory, and financial health of decentralized autonomous organizations.

5.4 New Valuation Models for DAOs

The previous sections highlighted the critical limitations of traditional valuation metrics when applied to DAOs and explored the insights offered by established network theories.

While these theories provide a valuable conceptual foundation, the unique dynamics of decentralized organizations demand a more tailored approach.

This chapter introduces a comprehensive valuation framework specifically designed for DAOs.

Building on network theory while incorporating effective participation analysis, governance efficiency, and real-world economic outputs, the proposed model aims to capture both the structural and functional dimensions of DAO value creation.

The framework is structured around a set of original Key Performance Indicators (KPIs), offering a multidimensional and pragmatic tool for assessing the sustainability, vitality, and economic impact of decentralized organizations.

5.4.1 Framework Overview

The valuation of DAOs requires a multidimensional approach that goes beyond traditional financial metrics and simple network size indicators.

An effective model must capture not only the structural aspects of the network (number of users, connections, subgroups) but also the quality of participation, the efficiency of governance mechanisms, and the ability to generate sustainable economic outputs. The proposed framework integrates three main analytical dimensions.

1. Network value metrics

Based on adapted interpretations of Metcalfe's Law, Reed's Law, and Beckstrom's Law, this dimension captures the scale, connectivity, and efficiency benefits generated by the DAO's network structure.

2. Participation and governance metrics

Recognizing that not all users contribute equally, this dimension focuses on active participation rates, voting behavior, proposal activity, delegation patterns, and governance responsiveness.

3. Economic output metrics

This dimension evaluates the tangible outcomes produced by the DAO, including funded projects, returns on treasury investments, user retention, innovation outputs, and measurable savings generated through decentralized operations.

Each dimension is operationalized through a set of KPIs specifically designed to be observable, measurable, and comparable across different types of DAOs. Together, these dimensions aim to provide a holistic and pragmatic evaluation tool, supporting both academic analysis and real-world decision-making by investors, developers, and DAO communities.

The following sections will detail the design of each dimension, the selection of KPIs, and the methodological principles underpinning the overall framework.

5.4.2 Network Value Metrics

The first dimension of the proposed valuation framework focuses on the structural value of a DAO's network. Network value metrics aim to quantify the potential and realized value generated by the size, connectivity, and interaction dynamics within the DAO.

This dimension draws from three foundational theories, Metcalfe's Law, Reed's Law, and Beckstrom's Law, each offering a different lens to assess network-driven value creation.

5.4.2.1 Metcalfe's Law Adaptation: Weighted Connection Value

Metcalfe's Law traditionally states that the value of a network grows proportionally to the square of the number of its nodes (n^2). However, in the context of DAOs, where participation is often uneven, a direct application of this law would overestimate the real value.

Thus, we propose a Weighted Metcalfe Model, where the number of active participants (rather than total token holders) is used:

$$Network\ Value \propto (n_{active})^2$$

Where:

- n_{active} represents wallets that have participated in governance activities (voting, proposal submission) within a defined time frame.
- α is a scaling factor representing the average value per pairwise connection between active participants.

Key Metric

Active participation square index (APSI): Measures the square of active participants as a proxy for network engagement value.

5.4.2.2 Reed's Law Adaptation: Effective Subgroup Formation

Reed's Law emphasizes the exponential growth of value based on the formation of subgroups (2^n). In DAOs, the creation of working groups, committees, or project-specific task forces can be a powerful indicator of dynamic value generation.

However, not all subgroups contribute equally. Therefore, we introduce the concept of Effective Subgroup Formation, counting only subgroups that meet minimum activity and impact criteria (e.g., number of proposals submitted, tasks completed).

Key Metric
Effective subgroup count (ESC): Number of active and productive subgroups relative to total membership.

5.4.2.3 Beckstrom's Law Adaptation: Economic Efficiency Gain
Beckstrom's Law suggests that network value is the sum of cost savings achieved by its members. For DAOs, this involves analyzing:

- Reduction in governance and operational costs.
- Automation of trust through smart contracts.
- Minimization of intermediary fees.

Given the complexity of measuring all these elements directly, a proxy can be developed based on:

$$Estimated\,Efficiency\,Gain = \frac{DAO\ Treasury\ Operational\ Costs}{Comparable\ Traditional\ Structure\ Costs}$$

Key Metric
Economic efficiency ratio (EER): Ratio comparing DAO operating costs to estimated costs of an equivalent centralized organization.

5.4.2.4 Synthesis of Network Value Metrics
To provide a robust evaluation, the three network value metrics (APSI, ESC, EER) can be normalized and combined into a CNVS.

This score offers a synthetic, yet multidimensional, indicator of the DAO's structural and interaction-driven value.

$$CNVS = \propto \times APSI + \beta \times ESC + \gamma \times ERR$$

Where α, β, and Υ are weights adjustable based on the specific nature and strategic goals of the DAO under analysis. In particular, the weighting process should consider:

- Strategic priorities: If a DAO prioritizes rapid subgroup formation and collaboration (e.g., innovation hubs, grant DAOs), greater weight should be assigned to the effective subgroup count (ESC),
- Operational model: DAOs heavily focused on economic efficiency (e.g., decentralized finance protocols) may prioritize the economic efficiency ratio (EER),
- Engagement objectives: In communities where participation and connection density are key (e.g., social DAOs), the active participation square index (APSI) should carry a higher weight.

The final weighting scheme can be determined through one or a combination of the following methods:

1. Expert judgment + structured scoring: It's a method widely used in practices such as multi-criteria decision analysis (MCDA). How it works:

   - A small group of experts (e.g., DAO founders, active users, developers, investors) is selected.
   - Each expert is asked to assign a relative importance score to each evaluation factor (e.g., on a 1–5 scale).
   - The scores are normalized to obtain the weights α, β, and γ, which should sum to 1.

Practical example: if experts assess active participation as 50% important, subgroup formation as 30%, and economic efficiency as 20%, the resulting weights would be:

$$\alpha = 0.5,\ \beta = 0.3, \gamma = 0.2$$

2. Analytic hierarchy process (AHP): A more mathematical and rigorous method, invented by Thomas Saaty. How it works:

   - Pairwise comparison matrices are constructed between evaluation criteria.
   - For example, participants evaluate how much more important active participation is compared to effective subgroup formation (on a 1–9 scale).

- Through eigenvalue calculation of the matrix, optimal weights are derived.

Pros:

- More objective and less prone to random bias.
- Formally accepted in scientific and operational research literature.

Cons: Requires more detailed data input and basic knowledge of linear algebra for computation.

3. Empirical calibration: A data-driven method based on real-world observations. How it works:

- Real DAO datasets are analyzed.
- Successful DAOs (e.g., those with growing treasuries, high retention rates) are examined to identify correlations between success indicators and the values of APSI, ESC, and EER.
- Weights are then derived based on observed statistical relationships.

Pros:

- Grounded in empirical evidence.
- Highly robust if sufficient historical data is available.

Cons:

- Requires extensive data collection and statistical analysis capabilities.
- Limited applicability if comparable datasets are scarce.

Selecting the most appropriate method depends on data availability, the maturity and type of the DAO under analysis, and the intended purpose of the valuation (academic research, strategic assessment, investment evaluation, etc.).

5.4.3 *Participation and Governance Metrics*

While network size and structure provide important insights into the potential value of a DAO, the actual engagement and behavior of its members are critical determinants of its operational effectiveness and long-term sustainability.

Participation and governance metrics aim to measure the intensity, quality, and resilience of the DAO's internal governance dynamics.

This dimension focuses on how actively members contribute to decision-making processes, how efficiently proposals are handled, and how governance mechanisms foster or hinder decentralized participation.

5.4.3.1 Active Participation Rate

A healthy DAO should maintain a robust level of active involvement from its members, particularly in governance activities such as voting and proposal submission.

Key Metric

Active participation rate (APR): The percentage of token holders (or eligible voters) who have participated in at least one governance action within a defined time frame (e.g., last 6 months).

$$APR = \frac{Number\ of\ active\ participants}{Total\ number\ of\ token\ holders} \times 100$$

5.4.3.2 Proposal Submission Rate

The dynamism of a DAO can also be gauged by the rate at which members submit new proposals, reflecting innovation, responsiveness, and internal engagement.

Key Metric

Proposal submission rate (PSR): The number of proposals submitted per 100 active members over a defined period.

5.4.3.3 Voting Efficiency and Participation Quorum

Beyond simply participating, the efficiency of voting processes, measured by participation quorum and voting turnout, is critical.

Key Metric

- Voting turnout ratio (VTR): The average percentage of eligible voters participating in governance votes.

- Quorum achievement rate (QAR): The proportion of proposals that meet the required quorum threshold.

5.4.3.4 Delegation Dynamics

Many DAOs implement delegation mechanisms, where token holders entrust their voting power to delegates. Analyzing delegation dynamics helps understand whether governance is truly participatory or excessively centralized among a few influential actors.

Key Metric

- Delegation concentration index (DCI): Measures the concentration of delegated voting power (e.g., Gini coefficient or similar concentration measures).
- Delegate participation rate (DPR): The proportion of delegates actively participating in votes and discussions relative to total appointed delegates.

5.4.3.5 Governance Responsiveness and Execution

Finally, governance is effective only if decisions translate into timely and tangible actions.

Key Metric

- Proposal implementation rate (PIR): The percentage of approved proposals actually implemented within a defined timeframe.
- Average execution time (AET): The average time between proposal approval and implementation.

5.4.3.6 Synthesis of Participation and Governance Metrics

The participation and governance metrics can be aggregated into a GHS, synthesizing active engagement, decision-making efficiency, delegation balance, and execution capability.

Each metric reflects a critical dimension of DAO governance dynamics, such as engagement, decision-making efficiency, proposal implementation, and delegation balance.

Table 5.1 summarizes the key components included in the GHS framework, along with a brief description, an example KPI, and an adjustable weight,

$\delta_1 - \delta_2 - \delta_3 \ldots$., reflecting the relative importance of each metric. The final GHS score is calculated as a weighted sum of these components,

Table 5.1 Key components included in the GHS framework and final GHS score

Metric	*Description*	*Example KPI*	*Weight* (δ_i)
Active participation rate (APR)	Percentage of token holders participating in governance activities	% of voters in last 6 months	δ_1
Proposal submission rate (PSR)	Rate of proposal submissions relative to active members	Proposals per 100 active members	δ_2
Voting turnout ratio (VTR)	Average turnout rate in governance votes	Average % of eligible voters participating	δ_3
Quorum achievement rate (QAR)	Percentage of proposals reaching the quorum	% of proposals meeting quorum requirements	δ_4
Proposal implementation rate (PIR)	Percentage of approved proposals implemented	% of implemented vs. approved proposals	δ_5
Average execution time (AET)	Average time between proposal approval and execution	Days from approval to execution	δ_6
Delegation concentration index (DCI)	Degree of concentration in delegated voting power	Gini coefficient of voting power	δ_7
Delegate participation rate (DPR)	Percentage of active delegates relative to total delegates	% of delegates voting regularly	δ_8
Weighted average (GHS)	**Composite governance score**	**Σ (Metric × Weight)**	**1.0**

allowing for tailored evaluation based on the strategic priorities and governance model of the specific DAO under analysis.

The weighting process can follow the same methodologies described previously, namely:

- Structured expert judgment: Gathering evaluations from DAO community leaders, governance facilitators, and active members to assign relative importance scores to each metric (e.g., active participation rate, proposal submission rate, voting turnout ratio).
- Analytic hierarchy process (AHP): Conducting pairwise comparisons among governance metrics to derive consistent weights through

eigenvalue analysis, ensuring logical coherence in the prioritization of participation and efficiency indicators.

- Empirical calibration: Analyzing governance data from comparable DAOs to observe which participation and governance factors most strongly correlate with long-term success metrics, such as proposal throughput, voter engagement, and decision implementation rates.

The selected method should align with the analytical goals of the evaluation, the nature of the DAO (e.g., small community-driven vs. large protocol governance), and the availability of internal governance data.

5.4.4 Economic Output Metrics

While network structure and governance health provide crucial insights into the vitality of a DAO, the ultimate measure of its sustainability and impact lies in its ability to generate tangible economic outcomes. Economic Output Metrics focus on assessing the real-world productivity, financial management, and value creation capabilities of decentralized organizations. This dimension aims to capture the DAO's capacity to deploy its resources effectively, support meaningful projects, retain active contributors, and ultimately contribute to the broader ecosystem it serves.

5.4.4.1 Treasury Management Efficiency

A key indicator of a DAO's economic maturity is the efficient and strategic management of its treasury assets.

Key Metric

- Treasury growth rate (TGR): Percentage change in the DAO's treasury balance over a given period, adjusted for external token price fluctuations.
- Treasury utilization rate (TUR): Percentage of treasury funds actively allocated to investments, grants, or operations, versus idle holdings.
- Treasury diversification index (TDI): Measures the spread of treasury assets across multiple asset classes (e.g., stablecoins, governance tokens, NFTs), reducing exposure to single-point risks.

5.4.4.2 *Project and Grant Output*

DAOs often finance external projects, internal initiatives, or grants. The success and impact of these funded activities reflect directly on the DAO's economic performance.

Key Metric

- Funded project success rate (FPSR): Percentage of funded projects that achieve predefined milestones or deliverables.
- Grant-to-output ratio (GOR): Ratio between grants awarded and tangible outputs produced (e.g., publications, software releases, product launches).
- Average funding efficiency (AFE): Average cost per successful project or deliverable achieved.

5.4.4.3 *Contributor Retention and Growth*

Long-term economic output depends heavily on the DAO's ability to attract and retain skilled contributors.

Key Metric

- Contributor retention rate (CRR): Percentage of contributors who remain active over consecutive governance cycles.
- Contributor growth rate (CGR): Percentage increase in the number of active contributors over a given period.
- Core contributor stability index (CCSI): Measures the persistence of key contributors (those with high governance or operational activity) over time.

5.4.4.4 *Ecosystem Impact*

Beyond internal productivity, a DAO's broader impact on its ecosystem is a significant indicator of long-term value creation.

Key Metric

- Partnership expansion rate (PER): Number of strategic partnerships or ecosystem collaborations formed over a period.
- Innovation index (II): Proxy measure of the DAO's contribution to new technologies, models, or standards within its domain (e.g., number of open-source projects initiated).
- Ecosystem funding ratio (EFR): Percentage of treasury or operational funds allocated to external ecosystem initiatives.

5.4.4.5 Synthesis of Economic Output Metrics

Similar to the approach used for network value and governance health, the various economic output metrics can be aggregated into a composite EOS.

Each metric is assigned a weight (δ_i) reflecting its relative importance in light of the DAO's mission, strategic priorities, and operating model.

The weights must satisfy the standard condition:

$$EOS = \sum_{i=1}^{n} \delta_i = 1$$

The resulting EOS offers a comprehensive and normalized measure of a DAO's productivity, operational sustainability, and overall capacity to generate economic value.

5.5 Toward an Integrated Framework for DAO Valuation

5.5.1 Rationale for an Integrated Approach

Valuing a DAO requires moving beyond traditional, single-dimensional evaluation methods. Unlike conventional corporations, where metrics such as revenue, net income, or asset base can provide relatively direct proxies for value, DAOs are multi-faceted entities whose strength lies in the dynamic interplay between their network structure, governance processes, and economic outputs.

A valuation model that focuses solely on one aspect, whether it be token price, treasury size, or number of members, risks misrepresenting the true resilience, sustainability, and value-creation potential of the organization.

In particular:

- A large network without active participation or effective governance can be fragile and inert.
- A governance system with high participation but poor economic management can lead to resource depletion without lasting impact.
- A strong treasury without dynamic community engagement and decision-making processes risks stagnation and decline.

Each pillar, network, governance, and economic output, contributes uniquely and interactively to the DAO's overall health and sustainability. An integrated valuation framework is therefore necessary to:

- Capture the complexity of decentralized systems.
- Balance quantitative and qualitative indicators of performance.
- Support informed decision-making by investors, participants, and strategic partners.
- Provide flexible and adaptable evaluation tools suitable for the diverse typologies of DAOs (DeFi protocols, social DAOs, grant organizations, etc.).

Only by integrating these dimensions into a comprehensive model can we realistically assess a DAO's current state and future potential, moving beyond simplistic snapshots toward dynamic, actionable insights.

5.5.2 Construction of the Composite DAO Valuation Model

Following the rationale for an integrated approach, the proposed DAO valuation model is constructed by aggregating three core dimensions:

- Network Value Score (CNVS)
- Governance Health Score (GHS)
- Economic Output Score (EOS)

Each dimension captures a critical aspect of the DAO's vitality and sustainability:

- CNVS measures the structural strength and interaction potential of the network.
- GHS assesses the efficiency, resilience, and inclusiveness of the governance processes.
- EOS reflects the tangible productivity and economic outcomes achieved by the DAO.

To ensure comparability and avoid distortions, each dimension is normalized to a common scale (e.g., from 0 to 1). Normalization allows the three scores to be meaningfully aggregated without biasing the composite valuation toward any specific metric simply due to differences in measurement scales. Each of the three scores is assigned a weight (δ) reflecting its relative importance in the specific DAO context:

- δ_{CNVS} for Network Value Score.
- δ_{GHS} for Governance Health Score.
- δ_{EOS} for Economic Output Score.

The weights must satisfy the standard condition:

$$\delta_{CNVS} + \delta_{GHS} + \delta_{EOS} = 1$$

This ensures that the composite score remains balanced and interpretable. Weighting factors allow the valuation model to remain flexible and adaptive to the DAO's strategic orientation:

- For a DeFi protocol, economic outputs may be weighted more heavily.
- For a grant DAO, governance health may have greater relevance.
- For a social DAO, network vitality and community engagement may be prioritized.

The composite DAO valuation model thus respects the diversity of DAO types while offering a standardized framework for evaluation.

5.5.3 Aggregated DAO Valuation Score (DVS)

Building upon the three core dimensions of DAO evaluation, Network Value, Governance Health, and Economic Output, the aggregated DVS provides a unified, comprehensive measure of a DAO's overall sustainability, resilience, and value-creation potential. The DVS is calculated as a weighted average of the normalized scores for each dimension:

$$DVS = \delta_{CNVS} \times CNVS + \delta_{GHS} \times GHS + \delta_{EOS} \times EOS$$

Where:

CNVS = Composite Network Value Score,
GHS = Governance Health Score,
EOS = Economic Output Score,

δ_{CNVS}—δ_{GHS}—δ_{EOS} are the respective weighting factors, satisfying:

$$\delta_{CNVS} + \delta_{GHS} + \delta_{EOS} = 1$$

Each weight can be customized based on the DAO's mission, structure, and strategic priorities, allowing for a flexible application across a wide range of decentralized organizations.

5.5.3.1 *Interpretation of the DVS*

The DVS offers a normalized score (typically between 0 and 1) that captures the multi-dimensional health and sustainability of the DAO. Higher DVS values indicate stronger structural networks, healthier governance dynamics, and more effective economic output generation. Interpretation guidelines may include:

DVS Range:	Interpretation
0.80–1.00:	Excellent—Highly sustainable and resilient DAO
0.60–0.79:	Good—Robust but with areas for improvement
0.40–0.59:	Moderate—Needs significant strengthening
0.20–0.39:	Weak—Major governance or economic vulnerabilities
0.00–0.19:	Critical—Unsustainable in current form

These thresholds are indicative and may be adapted based on sector-specific benchmarks or DAO typology.

5.5.3.2 *Flexibility and Customization*

While the model provides a standardized structure, it remains highly customizable:

- Flexible weighting: Weights can be adjusted to emphasize the dimensions most critical for a given DAO's purpose (e.g., governance for grant DAOs, economic output for DeFi protocols).
- Modular updates: As new data sources, governance models, or economic mechanisms emerge, the individual KPIs feeding into CNVS, GHS, and EOS can be updated without altering the overall framework structure.

Comparability: The model enables relative benchmarking among DAOs of similar types, supporting research, investment decisions, and ecosystem development.

5.5.4 *Practical Considerations and Limitations*

While the Composite DAO Valuation Model (DVS) provides a structured and multidimensional framework for assessing decentralized organizations, it is important to acknowledge certain practical considerations and inherent limitations.

5.5.4.1 Data Availability and Quality

The model relies heavily on the availability of reliable, up-to-date data related to network activity, governance processes, and economic outputs. In many DAOs, data may be fragmented, inconsistent, or difficult to extract, particularly when operations are spread across multiple platforms or when on-chain governance is supplemented by off-chain coordination (e.g., Discord, forums, Snapshot proposals without on-chain execution).

Efforts to standardize data collection and reporting will be crucial to ensure accurate and meaningful evaluations over time.

5.5.4.2 Subjectivity in Weight Assignments

While the model allows flexible weighting of dimensions to adapt to specific DAO contexts, the selection of weights inevitably introduces an element of subjectivity. Stakeholders may assign different importance levels to network vitality, governance health, or economic productivity based on strategic preferences, risk tolerance, or ideological commitments. To mitigate this, transparent documentation of weighting choices and sensitivity analyses across different scenarios are recommended.

5.5.4.3 Diversity of DAO Typologies

DAOs are a heterogeneous class of organizations, ranging from DeFi protocols to artistic collectives, social movements, and investment syndicates. No single valuation model can perfectly accommodate all variations without some level of contextual adjustment. The model presented here is intended to provide a generalizable foundation, but specific implementations should be tailored to the mission, size, maturity, and operational model of the DAO being evaluated.

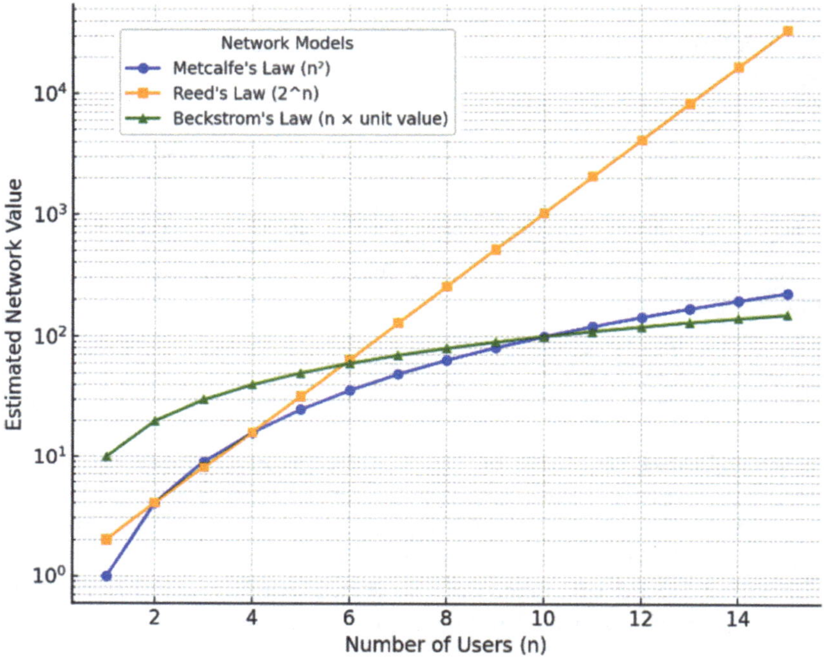

Fig. 5.2 Comparative growth curves of network value models

5.5.4.4 Evolution of DAO Governance and Technologies

The DAO landscape is dynamic, with rapid experimentation in governance mechanisms (e.g., quadratic voting, conviction voting, delegated governance) and economic structures (e.g., bonding curves, liquidity mining, retroactive funding). Metrics and evaluation models must therefore remain flexible and subject to revision as new paradigms emerge.

Periodic recalibration of KPIs, weighting schemes, and interpretation thresholds will be necessary to keep valuation models aligned with technological and organizational innovation.

5.5.4.5 Legal and Regulatory Ambiguity

DAOs operate in a legal grey area in many jurisdictions. The absence of formal legal recognition can affect how value is perceived, protected, or enforceable in case of disputes, treasury claims, or regulatory interventions. Valuation models should be interpreted within the context of this

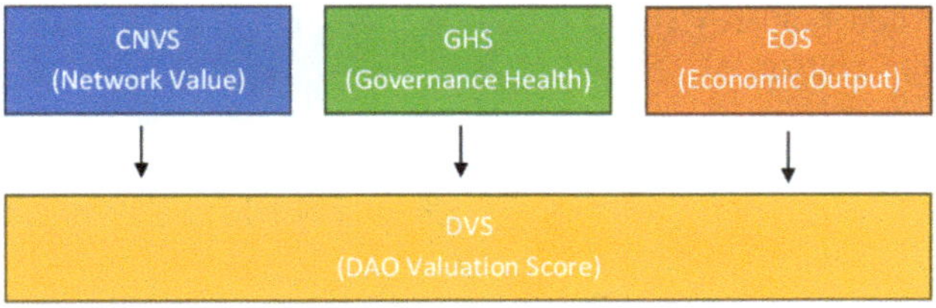

Fig. 5.3 Composite DAO Valuation Model (DVS). This diagram illustrates the integration of three core dimensions, CNVS (network value), GHS (governance health), and EOS (economic output) into a unified metric: the DVS. Each dimension contributes distinct evaluative insight, enabling a holistic assessment of DAO sustainability

regulatory uncertainty, recognizing that legal risks can materially impact the practical realizability of economic value.

Despite these limitations, developing structured, multidimensional valuation frameworks for DAOs is a critical step toward professionalizing decentralized governance, supporting informed decision-making, and enabling responsible investment and participation in the emerging Web3 ecosystem. Continuous refinement, open methodological debate, and empirical validation will be essential to advancing the quality and reliability of DAO valuation models over time.

The combined evaluation of these three pillars—network activity, governance quality, and economic output, forms the foundation for an integrated valuation methodology.

As illustrated in Fig. 5.2, this framework culminates in a composite metric that synthesizes the distinct dimensions into a unified DVS (Fig. 5.3).

5.6 Empirical Illustration: Valuing a Grant DAO

5.6.1 Selection Criteria for the Case Study

Grant DAOs represent one of the most strategically significant and rapidly evolving categories within the decentralized governance ecosystem. Their primary mission, allocating resources to public goods, community-driven projects, or innovation initiatives, makes them ideal candidates for testing multidimensional valuation frameworks.

Several factors justify the choice of a grant DAO as the subject of this empirical illustration:

- Governance-centric operations: Decision-making processes in grant DAOs are critical, involving funding allocations that directly reflect the community's collective priorities.
- Economic output visibility: Funded projects typically generate tangible outputs (e.g., open-source software, community initiatives, educational programs) that can be assessed for impact and efficiency.
- Network effects: Grant DAOs depend heavily on active participation, collaboration, and subgroup formation to identify, evaluate, and support grant recipients.
- Strategic relevance: The challenges and opportunities faced by grant DAOs closely align with the strategic design principles of emerging decentralized funding platforms, including EmpowerX.

Given these characteristics, a grant DAO offers a highly relevant and illustrative environment for applying and validating the proposed DAO valuation framework.

5.6.2 *Brief Profile of the Example DAO*

For this illustration, we consider a generic grant DAO based on common operational patterns observed in the decentralized funding sector, without directly replicating or analyzing a specific existing organization.

The generic grant DAO is characterized by:

- Mission: To fund community-driven innovation projects that contribute to the growth and sustainability of the decentralized ecosystem.
- Governance structure: Token-weighted voting on grant proposals, with optional delegation mechanisms to enhance participation rates.
- Treasury management: Managed in stablecoins and governance tokens, with a quarterly allocation budget for grants.
- Participation metrics: A moderately active governance community with approximately 1000 token holders, of which 15–20% actively participate in voting and proposal discussions.

- Economic outputs: Grants awarded to open-source developers, education initiatives, ecosystem builders, and DAO tooling projects, with an average project success rate of 70%.

This simplified profile enables the application of the valuation framework in a realistic but manageable context, illustrating how each pillar, network structure, governance health, and economic output, contributes to the overall valuation of a decentralized funding organization.

5.6.3 *Application of the Framework*

Applying the composite DAO valuation model to the generic grant DAO involves calculating each of the three pillar scores, CNVS, GHS, and EOS, using simplified illustrative data.

Normalization is assumed, meaning all scores are scaled between 0 and 1.

5.6.3.1 Network Value Score (CNVS)

Key observations:

- Approximately 1000 token holders.
- Active participation by 15–20% of holders.
- Several active working groups dedicated to grant evaluation and project mentoring.

Metric summary:

- Active participation square index (APSI): $(n_{active})^2$ normalized = 0.65.
- Effective subgroup count (ESC): 8 active subgroups normalized = 0.70.
- Economic efficiency ratio (EER): DAO treasury management efficiency normalized = 0.60.

Composite CNVS calculation

Assuming equal weights across APSI, ESC, and EER for simplicity:

$$CNVS = \frac{0.65 + 0.70 + 0.60}{3} = 0.65$$

5.6.3.2 *Governance Health Score (GHS)*

Key observations:

- Voter turnout averaging 18%.
- Delegation mechanisms in place but used by only 25% of token holders.
- High quorum achievement rate for grant funding proposals.

Metric summary:

- Active participation rate (APR): 0.18 normalized = 0.5.
- Proposal submission rate (PSR): Moderate = 0.55.
- Voting turnout ratio (VTR): 18% turnout normalized = 0.50.
- Proposal implementation rate (PIR): 95% of approved grants implemented = 0.90.
- Delegate participation rate (DPR): Low use = 0.40.

Composite GHS calculation:

Assuming a higher weight is assigned to PIR (execution quality), and moderate weights to the other metrics, we apply the following distribution:

- $\delta_{\text{APR}} = 0.15$
- $\delta_{\text{PSR}} = 0.15$
- $\delta_{\text{VTR}} = 0.15$
- $\delta_{\text{PIR}} = 0.40$
- $\delta_{\text{DPR}} = 0.15$

Applying the weights:

$$GHS = (0.15 \times 0.50) + (0.15 \times 0.55) + (0.15 \times 0.50) + (0.40 \times 0.90) + (0.15 \times 0.40)$$

$$GHS = 0.075 + 0.0825 + 0.075 + 0.36 + 0.06 = 0.6525$$

$$\text{Normalized GHS} \approx 0.65$$

5.6.3.3 Economic Output Score (EOS)

Key observations:

- Average project success rate: 70%.
- Grant-to-output ratio (GOR): Moderate, average funding efficiency.
- Contributor retention rate (CRR): Relatively high (repeat participation).

Metric summary:

- Funded project success rate (FPSR): 0.70
- Grant-to-output ratio (GOR): 0.60
- Contributor retention rate (CRR): 0.75
- Composite EOS calculation: 0.683

Composite EOS calculation

Assuming equal weights across the three metrics, the composite EOS is calculated as the normalized mean value of FPSR, GOR and CRR:

$$EOS = \frac{FPSR + GOR + CRR}{3} = \frac{0.70 + 0.60 + 0.75}{3} = 0.683$$

5.6.3.4 Aggregated DAO Valuation Score (DVS)

Assuming equal weights across CNVS, GHS, and EOS for simplicity:

$$\left(\delta_{CNVS} + \delta_{GHS} + \delta_{EOS} = \frac{1}{3}\right)$$

Substituting the normalized scores:

$$DVS = \left(\frac{1}{3} \times 0.65\right) + \left(\frac{1}{3} \times 0.65\right) + \left(\frac{1}{3} \times 0.683\right)$$

$$DVS = 0.2167 + 0.2167 + 0.2277 = 0.661$$

$$\text{Final DVS} \approx 0.66$$

Thus, the aggregated DVS for the generic grant DAO is approximately 0.661, indicating a moderately strong and balanced performance across network structure, governance health, and economic outputs. This result will be further interpreted and contextualized in the next section.

5.6.4 Interpretation of Results

The Aggregated DVS calculated for the generic grant DAO is approximately 0.661, placing the organization within the "Good" range according to the interpretive thresholds established in Chap. 4.

This result indicates a moderately strong and balanced performance across all three key dimensions:

- Network value: A relatively high level of active participation and effective subgroup formation, although not maximized across the full membership base.
- Governance health: Solid governance processes with a high rate of proposal implementation, tempered by relatively modest voter turnout and limited use of delegation mechanisms.
- Economic output: Consistent generation of tangible outputs through funded projects, with a healthy contributor retention rate, although some inefficiencies remain in grant-to-output ratios.

Overall, the DVS suggests that the generic grant DAO demonstrates sustainable operations, resilient governance, and positive economic impact, but with opportunities for improvement in expanding active participation and enhancing governance engagement structures.

5.7 Conclusion

This chapter has proposed a multidimensional framework for the valuation of DAOs, integrating network structure analysis, governance health evaluation, and economic output measurement.

The need for such a comprehensive model arises from the unique characteristics of DAOs, which challenge traditional business valuation paradigms by operating without centralized legal structures, relying instead on decentralized coordination and digital governance mechanisms.

Through the development of the composite DVS, we have demonstrated how it is possible to systematically assess a DAO's sustainability, resilience, and value-creation potential.

The empirical illustration, applying the model to a representative grant DAO, shows that this approach can produce actionable insights, highlighting organizational strengths and areas for strategic improvement.

While the model offers a flexible and adaptable framework, it also acknowledges inherent limitations related to data availability, subjectivity in weight assignment, typological diversity among DAOs, and the evolving nature of decentralized governance technologies.

Continuous refinement, empirical validation, and contextual adaptation will be essential to further improve the robustness and applicability of DAO valuation models in the future.

Ultimately, advancing structured valuation methodologies is crucial not only for investors, researchers, and governance participants, but also for the broader credibility, accountability, and sustainable growth of the decentralized ecosystem.

As DAOs continue to expand their influence across economic, social, and technological domains, rigorous and dynamic valuation frameworks will play an increasingly central role in supporting responsible decision-making and ecosystem development.

5.8 Design Takeaways: Valuation Insights for DAO Assessment

Strengths identified

- High alignment between governance outputs and project execution.
- Effective use of working groups to convert proposals into measurable outcomes.

Observed gaps

- Suboptimal engagement in governance processes limits the representativeness of collective decisions.
- Limited experimentation with advanced voting and delegation mechanisms reduces structural adaptability.

Valuation-relevant recommendations

- Incorporate governance activity metrics into DAO valuation frameworks (e.g., DHI).
- Monitor execution-to-approval ratios to assess operational efficiency.
- Include treasury composition and deployment patterns in economic sustainability analysis.
- Encourage modular governance to support long-term network resilience and investor confidence.

Appendix: Glossary of Key Metrics

1. Network Value Metrics

Acronym	*Metric name*	*Definition*
APSI	Active participation square index	Square of the number of active participants in governance, inspired by Metcalfe's Law
ESC	Effective subgroup count	Number of active subgroups or working groups that meet defined criteria for activity and productivity
EER	Economic efficiency ratio	Ratio comparing DAO operating costs to estimated costs of a comparable centralized organization

2. Governance Health Metrics

Acronym	*Metric name*	*Definition*
APR	Active participation rate	Percentage of token holders who have engaged in at least one governance action in a defined period
PSR	Proposal submission rate	Number of governance proposals submitted per 100 active members
VTR	Voting turnout ratio	Average percentage of eligible voters participating in governance votes
QAR	Quorum achievement rate	Percentage of proposals reaching the quorum threshold required for execution
PIR	Proposal implementation rate	Percentage of approved proposals that are implemented

(continued)

(continued)

Acronym	*Metric name*	*Definition*
AET	Average execution time	Average time elapsed between proposal approval and implementation
DCI	Delegation concentration index	Measure of how concentrated delegated voting power is (e.g., via Gini coefficient)
DPR	Delegate participation rate	Percentage of delegates who actively participate in governance

3. Economic Output Metrics

Acronym	*Metric name*	*Definition*
FPSR	Funded project success rate	Percentage of funded projects that achieve defined success milestones
GOR	Grant-to-output ratio	Ratio of total grant funding awarded to measurable project outcomes
AFE	Average funding efficiency	Average cost per successfully completed funded project or deliverable
CRR	Contributor retention rate	Percentage of contributors who remain active over consecutive periods
CGR	Contributor growth rate	Rate at which new contributors join the DAO over time
CCSI	Core contributor stability index	Measure of the persistence of key contributors over time
PER	Partnership expansion rate	Number of new strategic partnerships or collaborations per period
II	Innovation index	Proxy for the DAO's output of new models, products, or ideas
EFR	Ecosystem funding ratio	Share of treasury allocated to initiatives outside the DAO's internal operations

References

Buterin, V. (2017) '*DAOs, DACs, DAs and More: An Incomplete Terminology Guide*', Ethereum Blog. Available at: https://blog.ethereum.org/2014/05/06/daos-dacs-das-and-more/

Choudhury, S., & Koens, L. (2023). *A Framework for DAO Evaluation: Insights from Governance Analytics*. [Working Paper].

Coase, R. H. (1937). The nature of the firm. *Economica*, *4*(16), 386–405.
Cong, L. W., He, Z., & Li, J. (2021). Tokenomics: Dynamic adoption and valuation. *The Review of Financial Studies*, *34*(3), 1105–1155.
DeepDAO. (n.d.). *Analytics for Decentralized Autonomous Organizations*. https://deepdao.io/
De Filippi, P., & Wright, A. (2018). *Blockchain and the Law: The Rule of Code*. Harvard University Press.
Gitcoin DAO Governance Forum. https://gov.gitcoin.co/
Hassan, S., Reijers, W., & Wiertz, C. (2021). Decentralized autonomous organization: Governance and power in the digital society. *Big Data and Society*, *8*(1).
Nouns DAO Portal. https://nouns.wtf/
Optimism Collective Governance Hub. https://gov.optimism.io/
Ostrom, E. (1990). *Governing the Commons: The Evolution of Institutions for Collective Action*. Cambridge University Press.
Reijers, W., & Coeckelbergh, M. (2018). The blockchain as a narrative technology: Investigating the social ontology and normative configurations of cryptocurrencies'. *Philosophy and Technology*, *31*(1), 103–130.
Snapshot Labs. (n.d.). *Snapshot Documentation*. https://docs.snapshot.org/
Tally. (n.d.). DAO Governance Analytics. https://www.tally.xyz/

CHAPTER 6

Beyond the Code: Gödel's Incompleteness and the Limits of Formal Governance in DAOs

6.1 Introduction

6.1.1 Code, Trust, and the Dream of Perfect Governance

In a book about decentralized autonomous organizations (DAOs), one might not expect to encounter the name of Kurt Gödel, the logician whose 1931 incompleteness theorems revolutionized our understanding of formal systems. And yet, it is precisely here that Gödel's legacy becomes crucial.

The core aspiration of many DAO architectures is the creation of systems that are trustless, complete, and self-sufficient, in other words, systems that no longer require human judgment, discretion, or oversight. Governance becomes code, rules become law, and institutions become protocols.

Gödel reminds us that this dream of closure is, in itself, a kind of illusion. No formal system, no matter how elegant or secure, can account for all the truths within its own framework (Gödel, 1931). Some truths will always lie beyond the reach of its rules. And some decisions, especially those involving ethics, crisis, or ambiguity, will always require interpretation, not just execution.

As illustrated in Fig. 6.1, the structural analogy between formal systems and DAO protocols highlights the shared limitations of codified logic. In

A. Cesaretti, *DAO Governance in Theory and Practice*,
https://doi.org/10.1007/978-3-032-09675-3_6

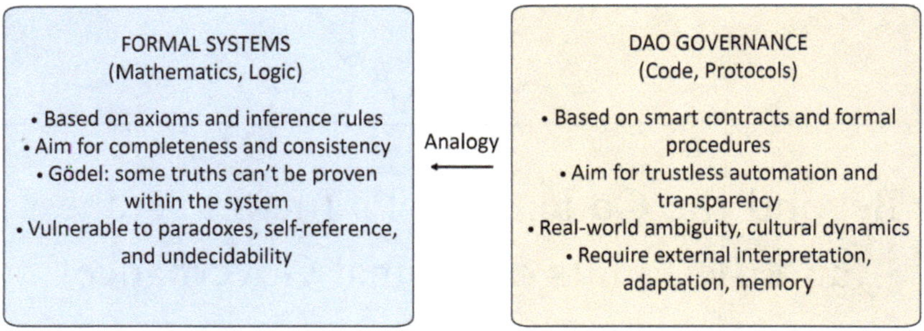

Fig. 6.1 Formal systems versus DAO governance: why incompleteness matters. A visual analogy between formal systems and DAO protocols: both rely on rule-based logic but face limits in addressing ambiguity and dissent. Just as Gödel revealed the incompleteness of formal systems, DAOs must integrate narrative and interpretation beyond the code to ensure sustainable governance

both cases, governance must go beyond rules to engage with interpretation, ambiguity, and evolving context.

This chapter is therefore not an academic detour, but a philosophical grounding for what follows. It affirms that those designing DAO governance systems are not merely writing code, they are constructing institutions. And true institutions, like human communities, must be capable of doubt, reflection, and adaptation. In the end, invoking Gödel here is not about rejecting formal governance.

It is about designing it with humility.

In the early days of blockchain, trust was replaced with code. The rallying cry "don't trust, verify" captured a bold aspiration: to build systems so transparent and deterministic that human discretion would become unnecessary. Smart contracts, immutable ledgers, and decentralized protocols offered a vision of governance free from ambiguity, corruption, and institutional failure. In this vision, rules would no longer need interpreters—they would simply execute.

Decentralized autonomous organizations (DAOs) embody this ambition. They promise communities that govern themselves through code, rather than through boards, bureaucracies, or political bodies. By automating collective decision-making via smart contracts, DAOs aim to transcend the messiness of human institutions with formal precision and algorithmic certainty.

But what if that very ambition carries within it a paradox?

Enter Kurt Gödel. In 1931, the young logician demonstrated that every formal system powerful enough to express arithmetic is, by its nature, incomplete. No matter how refined the logic, there will always be truths it cannot prove, and rules it cannot resolve from within. Gödel's Incompleteness Theorems shattered the dream of perfect formalization in mathematics. Yet their relevance extends far beyond logic and numbers.

This chapter begins with a simple question: can governance ever be complete?

Gödel's insights challenge us to reconsider the foundational assumptions of DAO design. They compel us to recognize that no matter how comprehensive a protocol appears, edge cases will emerge. Crises will arise that cannot be pre-coded. Conflicts will occur where the rules fall silent. And in those moments, governance cannot be purely formal, it must be interpretive, contextual, and adaptive.

In this sense, Gödel offers more than a critique. He offers a design principle: incompleteness is not a bug, it is a feature. It reminds us that truly resilient systems must remain open, not closed; flexible, not frozen. Trust may never be eliminated, but it can be restructured. Not into blind faith, but into deliberative processes, accountable layers, and community-led evolution.

DAO governance, then, is not the end of politics, it is its reconfiguration. And this reconfiguration begins not with code, but with humility.

6.1.2 *The Promise of DAO Governance: Transparency, Determinism, Trustlessness*

From their inception, DAOs have carried an extraordinary promise: the replacement of human discretion and institutional trust with the certainty of code. At the heart of this vision lies a powerful belief that governance, once enshrined in smart contracts, can become transparent, deterministic, and trustless.

Transparency in the DAO context means that rules, transactions, and decisions are publicly accessible and verifiable on-chain. Every action can be inspected, audited, and traced, eliminating the opacity that has historically plagued traditional institutions. In theory, this radical openness is a safeguard against corruption, favoritism, and arbitrary decisions.

Determinism refers to the idea that smart contracts, once deployed, execute precisely as written. Unlike human actors, code is supposed to be incorruptible, incapable of bias, and immune to external pressures. This determinism inspires confidence that outcomes are predictable and consistent, reducing the need for subjective interpretation.

Trustlessness represents perhaps the boldest aspiration of all. It proclaims that individuals can coordinate and transact without having to trust each other, or any central authority. Instead, trust is shifted to the code and to cryptographic guarantees. "Don't trust, verify" became the rallying cry of early blockchain communities, reflecting the belief that technology could eliminate the necessity for human trust altogether.

This vision resonates deeply with communities disillusioned by institutional failures, political corruption, and opaque corporate governance. For DAO advocates, trustlessness promises not only efficiency but liberation from the vulnerabilities of human institutions.

Yet this very promise carries within it the seeds of tension and paradox. For while code can execute predefined instructions flawlessly, it cannot interpret ambiguity, resolve ethical dilemmas, or adapt to unforeseen crises. Governance, ultimately, involves not only rule enforcement but also judgment, discretion, and sometimes mercy—qualities that escape the confines of deterministic code.

As we shall see in the coming sections, Gödel's insights remind us that even the most elegant formal systems are limited in their capacity to capture every possible truth or scenario. DAOs, built on rigid protocols, must confront the messy realities of human communities and the unpredictable nature of social dynamics. The dream of perfect governance through transparency, determinism, and trustlessness remains powerful—but incomplete.

6.1.3 The Belief in Formal Systems as a Replacement for Institutional Trust

One of the deepest convictions driving the design of DAOs is the belief that formal systems, rules encoded in smart contracts, can replace the fragile and often flawed trust we place in human institutions. In this view, law, governance, and even ethics can be reduced to programmable logic, removing the need for interpretation, discretion, or human judgment.

This belief has powerful roots. History is full of institutional betrayals: governments corrupted by special interests, corporations engaging in fraud, financial institutions collapsing under hidden risks. Each scandal reinforces the conviction that humans, even when acting under rules, remain unpredictable and fallible. The dream of blockchain technology is to eliminate these vulnerabilities by encoding rules that cannot be bent or selectively enforced (De Filippi & Wright, 2018).

Decentralized autonomous organizations (DAOs) embody this aspiration. They promise communities that governance can be mathematized, transformed into code that executes automatically, without bias or intervention. Smart contracts, once deployed, operate beyond manipulation. Decisions are recorded immutably on-chain, creating a ledger of absolute truth.

For many in the blockchain space, this vision is not merely technical but deeply philosophical. It reflects a faith in formalism: the notion that, given precise enough rules, social order can emerge without the need for trust in people. Governance becomes an engineering problem rather than a political or ethical challenge.

Yet this belief carries significant risks. As Gödel demonstrated, even the most sophisticated formal systems harbor limits and paradoxes. Rules cannot anticipate every possible situation. Ambiguity, interpretation, and judgment are not mere flaws, they are essential features of human governance.

When a DAO faces a crisis, an exploit, a contentious fork, or an unprecedented moral dilemma, code alone cannot decide what is fair, prudent, or legitimate. The rules may fall silent precisely when guidance is most needed. This is not merely a technical failure but a philosophical warning: formal systems can support governance, but they cannot fully replace the human processes of deliberation, negotiation, and moral choice.

The dream of replacing institutional trust with formal systems is seductive and partly achievable. Code can enforce consistency, transparency, and rule-following with unmatched precision. But as this chapter argues, true governance cannot be entirely automated. It must remain open to context, ambiguity, and human values.

Gödel's insights serve as a cautionary note: no system of rules can be complete unto itself. Any attempt to create perfectly self-sufficient governance will eventually collide with questions that lie beyond its coded boundaries. For DAOs to thrive, they must embrace this incompleteness, not as a defect to be eliminated, but as a design principle to be acknowledged and integrated.

6.1.4 *Why Gödel Matters in This Context*

This chapter uses Gödel's Incompleteness Theorems as philosophical and institutional metaphors rather than technical or mathematical analyses. While Gödel's results formally address limits in logical systems, here they serve as a conceptual lens for understanding why rule-based governance systems, including DAOs, can never be entirely complete or free from uncertainty. Readers should not interpret references to "incompleteness" as mathematical proofs applicable to blockchain protocols, but as an invitation to recognize that even the most precise rules cannot capture the full complexity of human decision-making and collective behavior.

6.2 Gödel's Incompleteness Theorems: A Primer for the Decentralized Era

6.2.1 *Historical Context: Formalism, Hilbert's Program, and the Crisis of Foundations*

In the early twentieth century, German mathematician David Hilbert launched an ambitious project: to formalize all of mathematics into a complete, consistent, and decidable system (Hilbert, 1928). This vision, now known as Hilbert's Program, aimed to provide absolute certainty through logic. Every mathematical truth, Hilbert believed, should be provable by a finite sequence of formal steps. The idea was to eliminate ambiguity, subjectivity, and paradox from the foundations of knowledge.

Gödel's 1931 incompleteness theorems shattered this dream. He proved that any formal system powerful enough to describe arithmetic is inherently incomplete: it contains truths that cannot be proven within its own rules, and it cannot demonstrate its own consistency from within its own rules. In essence, no system can fully capture its own logic without stepping outside itself.

This has profound resonance for the world of decentralized governance. Many DAOs echo the spirit of Hilbert's Program, aiming to encode all relevant rules, behaviors, and decisions into smart contracts that operate without ambiguity or exception. Yet, as Gödel showed, any system that aspires to formal perfection will encounter limits that cannot be resolved from within. Governance, like mathematics, must confront the inevitability of uncertainty and the need for external reflection.

Rather than discouraging the development of DAOs, Gödel's insight invites a more realistic, adaptive approach. It calls for flexibility, legitimacy beyond code, and the humility to recognize that even the most elegant protocol is not immune to incompleteness.

6.2.2 *The Core Idea: Truth Beyond Provability*

Gödel's Incompleteness Theorems revolve around a deceptively simple yet profound insight: there exist truths that cannot be proven within the systems designed to contain them.

In any sufficiently powerful formal system, one capable of expressing basic arithmetic, it is possible to construct statements that are true, but for which no proof exists inside the system's own rules. Such statements assert their own unprovability: they effectively say, "This sentence cannot be proven true within this system." If the system could prove them, it would become inconsistent; if it cannot, it remains incomplete. This analogy echoes Hofstadter's (1979) reflections on self-reference and the limits of formal systems in Goedel, Echer, Bach where recursive structures reveal how any rule-based system eventually points beyond itself.

This notion of truth beyond provability shattered the belief that logic alone could capture the entirety of mathematical reality. Gödel revealed that no formal structure can be both complete and consistent when it reaches a certain level of complexity.

While initially confined to the realm of mathematics, this insight has profound implications for any system that aspires to encode all possible truths or rules into a closed framework, including decentralized governance protocols.

6.2.3 *How Incompleteness Emerges in Systems Capable of Basic Arithmetic*

Gödel's results apply specifically to formal systems powerful enough to express elementary arithmetic, systems that can state and manipulate facts like "2 + 2 = 4." The reason is that, at this level of expressive power, systems gain the ability to talk about themselves.

Using clever logical encoding (now called Gödel numbering), Gödel showed that statements could represent claims about the system's own provability. The system gains a self-referential capacity, allowing it to express statements such as: "*This statement is not provable within this system.*"

If the system could prove that statement, it would contradict itself, implying it's both provable and unprovable, a paradox leading to inconsistency. If it cannot prove the statement, the system admits there is at least one true proposition it cannot prove, a sign of incompleteness.

Thus, the very power and expressiveness of formal systems sow the seeds of their own limits. The ability to encode rules, proofs, and meta-statements about the system itself inevitably introduces statements that lie just outside the system's reach.

6.2.4 The Analogy to Self-Governing Systems

The relevance of Gödel's insights extends far beyond mathematics and reaches directly into the world of decentralized governance and DAOs.

Decentralized autonomous organizations (DAOs) strive to encode all necessary rules and decision-making processes into smart contracts, creating governance systems that are deterministic, transparent, and trustless. The ambition is to design a protocol so complete and self-sufficient that no external discretion or interpretation would ever be needed.

Yet, as Gödel demonstrated, any system complex enough to describe and manage itself will eventually encounter scenarios it cannot fully resolve from within. Governance crises, ethical dilemmas, unforeseen attacks, or emergent conflicts often produce situations that lie outside the precise conditions anticipated by smart contracts. Rules can fall silent, leaving a void that no algorithm can fill.

Consider a DAO that encodes a detailed voting procedure for funding proposals. What happens if two conflicting proposals pass simultaneously due to timing or network delays? Or if a new regulatory development creates legal risks that the DAO was not programmed to handle? These "edge cases" are the governance equivalents of Gödelian statements: conditions the system cannot adjudicate purely from within its predefined rules.

Gödel's lesson, therefore, is not a rejection of formal governance, but a warning against the illusion of perfect closure. Self-governing systems, like formal systems, require mechanisms for interpretation, flexibility, and meta-level governance that can step outside the rigid code to resolve unforeseen conflicts.

Ultimately, the analogy invites DAO designers and communities to embrace the idea that incompleteness is not a flaw, it is an inevitable feature of any living, complex system. Rather than pursuing perfect formalization, sustainable decentralized governance must build in processes for reflection, human judgment, and adaptation.

6.3 DAOs as Formal Systems: Ambitions and Blind Spots

6.3.1 Smart Contracts as Closed Logical Systems

Smart contracts are often described as the ultimate realization of formal systems. They execute deterministic logic, free from human discretion, based solely on conditions encoded in their code. Once deployed, a smart contract behaves like a closed logical system: its outputs depend solely on its programmed rules and the inputs it receives.

This precision is both the strength and the core limitation of smart contracts. They are extraordinarily reliable for predictable scenarios. However, their very nature as closed systems makes them ill-suited for dealing with ambiguity, context, or moral judgment. Smart contracts cannot "interpret" intent, weigh ethical considerations, or navigate situations outside their predefined logic.

This is why many DAO governance mechanisms, although built on the promise of trustlessness and determinism, remain vulnerable to edge cases that no one anticipated, a reality echoing Gödel's insight that no formal system can be entirely self-sufficient.

6.3.2 Formal Verification, Consensus, and Immutability as Strengths and Limitations

DAOs rely on mechanisms like formal verification, cryptographic consensus, and immutability to guarantee security, correctness, and trust minimization. These elements provide a level of certainty unmatched by traditional institutions:

- Formal verification mathematically proves that smart contracts conform to specific properties or rules, reducing the risk of bugs.

- Consensus protocols ensure that network participants agree on a single version of truth, preserving consistency across distributed ledgers.
- Immutability guarantees that once data or code is written on-chain, it cannot be altered retroactively.

Yet these same strengths can become sources of rigidity.

- Formal proofs are only as complete as the specifications they check; unanticipated conditions remain outside their scope.
- Consensus can ossify around flawed rules, creating collective paralysis instead of adaptability.
- Immutability, while protecting integrity, can lock errors or suboptimal decisions into a protocol, leaving communities with few tools to correct them except contentious forks.

These limitations illustrate that even rigorously formalized systems carry blind spots. They cannot anticipate every contextual nuance or social dynamic, highlighting the need for meta-governance layers capable of adapting rules and resolving crises.

6.3.3 Case Studies of DAO Breakdowns or Forks Due to Unforeseen Edge Cases

The history of DAOs provides concrete examples of Gödelian incompleteness in action—moments where the formal system of rules proved insufficient to resolve critical issues from within.

The DAO Hack (2016)
One of the earliest and most famous examples is The DAO on Ethereum. Despite being lauded for its elegant smart contract design, it fell victim to an exploit not anticipated by its creators. The attacker used the contract's own logic to recursively withdraw funds, siphoning away millions of dollars. The smart contract followed the code perfectly. It simply failed to account for an unforeseen edge case.

The community faced an impossible choice:

- Respect immutability and accept the theft.
- Or intervene with a hard fork, rewriting history to undo the attack.

Ultimately, the fork was executed, splitting Ethereum into two chains: Ethereum (ETH) and Ethereum Classic (ETC). This crisis revealed that "code is law" collapses when law proves silent on unprecedented events.

MakerDAO Black Thursday (2020)
In March 2020, a sudden crash in crypto prices and network congestion led to zero-bid liquidations in MakerDAO's protocol. The system failed to properly handle extreme volatility, allowing liquidators to acquire collateral for negligible bids. Although not a smart contract bug, it exposed the limitations of governance parameters set in code without considering rare but catastrophic market conditions.

This event led to significant reforms in MakerDAO's risk models and governance processes, illustrating that formal rules must continuously evolve in response to external realities.

Other Examples

- Compound governance bug (2021): A proposal intended to update token distribution logic accidentally locked millions of dollars in rewards due to an overlooked code path. The community could not simply "fix the code" without deploying new contracts, revealing the inertia inherent in immutable protocols.
- SushiSwap leadership crisis: While not purely technical, this crisis demonstrated how social conflicts and personal dynamics can destabilize a DAO, even if the protocol's code remains untouched.

These cases collectively demonstrate that DAO governance cannot rely solely on formal logic. Crises often require human judgment, social negotiation, and adaptive mechanisms that exist beyond the code itself.

6.3.4 The Myth of "Code Is Law" as a Complete System

The slogan "code is law" has become one of the most iconic phrases in the blockchain space (Lessig, 2006). It captures the belief that rules encoded in software can replace legal systems, institutions, and discretionary human governance.

While compelling, this idea is fundamentally incomplete. Code can enforce certain behaviors with mechanical precision, but it cannot:

- Interpret ambiguous situations.
- Resolve ethical dilemmas.
- Weigh competing values or social interests.
- Adapt to external shocks without human intervention.

Gödel's Incompleteness Theorems serve as a philosophical lens to understand why "code is law" can never be fully sufficient. Formal rules are always bounded. Edge cases, exceptions, and unforeseen crises lie outside their deterministic framework.

This does not mean that code has no value in governance. It has extraordinary power to enhance transparency, consistency, and security. But elevating code to the level of a complete system of law ignores the essential human elements of interpretation, deliberation, and moral judgment.

The lesson for DAO designers is clear: code is an instrument, not an institution. Sustainable governance requires recognizing the limits of formal systems and designing mechanisms for human discretion, conflict resolution, and collective adaptation.

6.4 Incompleteness in Practice: Where DAOs Meet the Unknown

6.4.1 *Governance Crises: Decisions That the Code Cannot Resolve*

Decentralized autonomous organizations (DAOs) are often celebrated for their clarity and predictability, rooted in code that executes deterministic rules. Yet, time and again, DAOs have confronted moments when the code falls silent, when no line of logic or smart contract clause provides an answer.

Such governance crises emerge because not all future scenarios can be fully anticipated. Rules written today cannot foresee every technological failure, regulatory change, or community schism that may arise tomorrow. The problem is not merely technical, it is structural. As Gödel showed, even the most elegant formal systems harbor unprovable truths and edge cases that lie beyond their internal logic.

In DAOs, these crises manifest as:

- Disputes over how to interpret ambiguous rules.
- Conflicting proposals that both satisfy procedural criteria.
- Situations requiring ethical judgment rather than pure logic.

When crises hit, communities face a stark reality: governance cannot be purely automatic. It must remain capable of deliberation, negotiation, and human discretion.

6.4.2 *Moral or Strategic Dilemmas That Exceed Pre-written Rules*

Beyond technical bugs, DAOs also encounter moral and strategic dilemmas that defy resolution through code alone. These dilemmas often involve competing values, legitimate but conflicting interests, or trade-offs that no smart contract can adjudicate.

Examples include:

- Allocating community funds between high-risk innovation and conservative sustainability.
- Responding to regulatory pressure. Should a DAO comply, resist, or pivot?
- Censoring harmful content or actors while preserving principles of decentralization and free participation.

Such situations expose the limits of "code is law." Even with perfect foresight, no set of rules can encode values like fairness, proportionality, or moral judgment.

As Gödel teaches us, formal systems inevitably encounter truths they cannot decide from within. DAOs, too, must face decisions that require interpretation, compromise, and ethical reasoning.

6.4.3 *Need for Off-chain or Meta-layer Arbitration*

In practice, many DAOs have developed off-chain or meta-layer processes to address crises that their on-chain systems cannot handle. This creates a two-layer governance reality:

- The on-chain layer, where rules execute automatically.
- And the off-chain layer, where human discussion, negotiation, and decision-making take place.

Off-chain arbitration can take many forms:

- Emergency councils with limited powers,
- Informal forums for community consensus,
- Legal entities created to act on behalf of the DAO in regulatory contexts (Reijers and Coeckelbergh, 2018).

These meta-layer processes represent the DAO's adaptive immune system—the mechanism that steps in when formal rules are insufficient. Far from betraying the ethos of decentralization, they acknowledge that governance requires mechanisms for interpretation, flexibility, and crisis management.

This is not a weakness. It is a recognition that incompleteness is an inherent feature of any governance system. Even in decentralized environments, there must exist institutions, however informal, that can step outside the code to address exceptional circumstances.

6.4.4 Examples: The DAO (2016), MakerDAO Emergencies, Lido's Staking Debates

The DAO Hack (2016)

The DAO hack remains the most iconic example of governance hitting the limits of code. The smart contract operated precisely as written, yet an unforeseen exploit allowed funds to be drained. No on-chain mechanism existed to reverse the theft. The community had to decide whether to:

- Honor immutability and accept the loss.
- Or intervene with a hard fork.

Ultimately, Ethereum's fork created two chains: Ethereum and Ethereum Classic. This episode proved that code alone could not resolve the ethical and practical dilemma.

MakerDAO Black Thursday (2020)
During the March 2020 market crash, MakerDAO's systems failed to handle extreme volatility. Liquidations occurred at near-zero prices due to network congestion, leaving the protocol undercollateralized.

Despite having meticulously designed parameters, MakerDAO was forced to suspend certain operations and redesign its risk frameworks. The crisis revealed that:

- Market conditions can exceed any pre-set rules.
- Real-time human intervention was crucial for stabilizing the system.

Lido's Staking Debates
Lido, a leading staking protocol, has faced contentious debates over staking centralization. As Lido grows, so does its share of Ethereum's staking power, raising concerns about network security and decentralization.

Lido's DAO has struggled to decide:

- Whether to impose self-limits on market share,
- Or to allow growth unchecked.

The dilemma is not technical but strategic and ethical:

- Should the DAO prioritize its own dominance?
- Or act in the broader interest of Ethereum's decentralization?

No smart contract can answer these questions. The debate continues in forums, community calls, and governance proposals, a vivid illustration that some decisions cannot be automated.

These examples underscore a critical lesson: even the most advanced DAOs inevitably encounter situations where governance must transcend code and enter the realm of human judgment, negotiation, and collective wisdom.

Gödel's message resonates here powerfully: no system of rules is complete unto itself. Sustainable governance demands humility, the willingness to accept that formal systems, while powerful, will always encounter the unknown.

6.5 Toward Adaptive Governance: Embracing Incompleteness

6.5.1 *The Necessity of "Outside the System" Reasoning*

Gödel's Incompleteness Theorems teach a crucial lesson: no system can fully contain all truths about itself. There will always be statements or, in governance terms, situations that cannot be resolved purely from within the existing rules.

For DAOs, this insight translates into a simple but profound design principle: every governance system needs a mechanism to step outside its own framework. This "outside the system" reasoning is not a sign of failure. It is a recognition that rigid adherence to code can lead to deadlocks, injustices, or systemic crises when novel circumstances arise.

True institutional resilience requires channels for interpretation, deliberation, and context-sensitive decision-making. This is the foundation of adaptive governance.

6.5.2 *Meta-governance, Interpretative Councils, and Legitimacy Layers*

One of the most promising approaches to handling incompleteness in DAOs is the creation of meta-governance structures, mechanisms that sit above the routine execution of smart contracts.

These may include:

- Interpretative councils tasked with resolving edge cases or ambiguities.
- Emergency committees authorized to intervene during crises.
- Constitutional layers that define how the DAO can amend its own rules.

These meta-level institutions perform the critical role of translating community values into practical decisions when the code is silent. Yet they introduce their own risks: power concentration, lack of accountability, or the emergence of a new elite. To preserve legitimacy, DAOs must design these structures with:

- High transparency.
- Clear limits on authority.

- Mechanisms for community oversight or recall.

Meta-governance is not an abandonment of decentralization. Instead, it is a recognition that decentralization without interpretative capacity risks paralysis.

6.5.3 *Designing Flexibility Without Reintroducing Centralized Authority*

The paradox facing DAOs is clear: they need flexibility, but flexibility can quickly drift into centralized discretion if left unchecked.

Several design strategies can help balance these tensions:

- Rotating membership in interpretative bodies to prevent entrenchment.
- Procedural transparency, so that all deliberations and decisions are documented and open to scrutiny.
- Limited mandates, defining the specific conditions under which meta-governance bodies can act.
- Community veto mechanisms, allowing the broader DAO to override decisions perceived as illegitimate.

The goal is to embed humility into governance design: a recognition that some decisions will require human judgment, but that such judgment must remain accountable and contestable.

6.5.4 *Procedural Pluralism: Combining Algorithmic execution With Human Oversight*

A sustainable DAO governance system will likely embrace what can be called procedural pluralism: the combination of algorithmic execution and human oversight.

Algorithmic governance excels at routine operations:

- Allocating funds according to clear formulas.
- Enforcing quorum rules.
- Automating repetitive tasks.

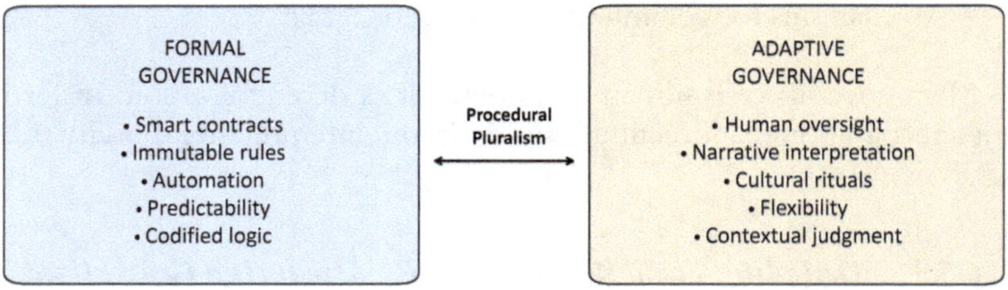

Fig. 6.2 Formal versus Adaptive Governance: A Procedural Pluralism Model. This diagram visualizes the coexistence of two complementary logics in DAO governance. On one side, formal mechanisms (smart contracts, automation) offer rule-based precision. On the other, adaptive elements (narratives, human oversight) provide flexibility, context-awareness, and resilience. Procedural pluralism bridges these dimensions to enable sustainable decentralized coordination

Human governance becomes essential when:

- Moral dilemmas arise.
- Unexpected crises demand interpretation.
- Rules conflict or fall silent.

Rather than seeing these two layers as mutually exclusive, procedural pluralism treats them as complementary. Code provides speed, precision, and consistency. Human deliberation provides context, adaptability, and ethical judgment.

Designing DAOs to operate across these two dimensions ensures that formal rules remain strong where they work best, while human communities can step in where the rules reach their limits. This approach transforms Gödel's insight into a practical design principle: incompleteness is not a flaw, but a feature to be embraced and integrated.

Gödel reminds us that no system can ever be entirely self-contained. For DAOs, the path forward lies not in the impossible pursuit of perfect formalization, but in building institutions capable of adapting, interpreting, and evolving. Adaptive governance is not merely a safeguard, it is the key to sustaining decentralized systems in a complex, unpredictable world (Fig. 6.2).

6.6 Conclusion: Decentralization With Humility

6.6.1 *Incompleteness is Not a Flaw, but a Feature of Systems Grounded in Reality*

Gödel's Incompleteness Theorems were a profound revelation not only for mathematics but for any system that aspires to formal perfection. They remind us that no set of rules, however elegant, can fully capture all truths or anticipate every scenario. Incompleteness is not a defect, it is the inevitable reality of complex, living systems (Floridi, 2014).

For DAOs, this insight is not a reason for pessimism but an invitation to design with humility. Recognizing that gaps will emerge makes governance more resilient, not weaker.

6.6.2 *DAO Governance Should Recognize the Limits of Formality*

The promise of DAOs has often been framed as the triumph of code over human discretion, a vision where transparency, determinism, and trustlessness would eliminate the failures of traditional institutions. Yet this very aspiration can become a blind spot.

Decentralized autonomous organization (DAO) governance should embrace the limits of formality. Formal rules can define processes, enforce accountability, and ensure consistency. But they cannot:

- Resolve moral dilemmas.
- Adapt to unforeseen crises.
- Interpret the spirit behind the letter of the rules.

Sustainable decentralized systems must incorporate mechanisms that allow communities to step outside the code when necessary.

6.6.3 *From Rigid Architecture to Living Protocol: Governance as Evolving Dialogue*

A DAO is not merely a technological artifact. It is a living institution. Governance should not be conceived as a rigid architecture to be perfected once and for all. Instead, it must remain an evolving dialogue, a space where rules, values, and social norms are continuously renegotiated.

Gödel's lesson points to the wisdom of designing systems that are:

- Open to amendment.
- Transparent in their interpretative processes.
- Capable of learning from crises and adapting over time.

DAOs that succeed will be those that see protocols not as frozen law, but as living documents, responsive to the unpredictable nature of human communities.

In this light, DAO governance architectures should be conceived not as finalized technical systems, but as adaptive frameworks that embed institutional memory, social negotiation, and epistemic humility.

6.6.4 A Call for Reflective, Responsible Decentralization

Decentralization is often portrayed as an absolute good, a panacea for corruption, inefficiency, and institutional failure. But decentralization itself is not immune to new forms of power, opacity, or dysfunction.

This chapter calls for a reflective, responsible:

- One that balances algorithmic precision with human judgment.
- One that acknowledges the risk of informal hierarchies even in decentralized settings.
- One that prioritizes legitimacy and adaptability over ideological purity.

True decentralization is not the absence of governance, it is the transformation of governance into a more transparent, participatory, and humble endeavor.

This vision echoes the broader argument of the book: that effective governance is not about closing complexity, but about creating structures capable of navigating it. From Gödel to adaptive protocols, from hybrid architectures to narrative legitimacy, the core strength of DAOs lies in their capacity to evolve while sustaining collective trust.

6.6.5 *Embracing Incompleteness: Why Hybrid DAOs are the Way Forward*

The path forward for DAOs lies in hybrid governance models that combine the strengths of code with the irreplaceable virtues of human deliberation.

Hybrid DAOs:

- Automate routine operations with smart contracts.
- But reserve space for community interpretation in complex or unforeseen situations.
- Create meta-governance layers to resolve without reverting to centralization.

Such systems reflect Gödel's essential message: incompleteness is inevitable—but it can be managed. By designing DAOs that anticipate their own limits, communities can avoid the twin perils of rigid formalism and unchecked human discretion.

DAOs of the future will not be purely algorithmic or purely social. They will be living systems, blending the clarity of code with the wisdom of collective judgment. Decentralization with humility is not a compromise, it is the only path to sustainable, resilient governance in a world where certainty will always remain incomplete.

The insights from Gödel's Incompleteness Theorems provide a conceptual foundation for the architectural approach developed here, which opens the path to the concrete design strategies and architectural blueprints explored in Chap. 7, where incompleteness becomes a resource for institutional innovation.

In this vision, governance is not a finished structure to be defended, but a landscape to be explored, iteratively, collectively, and with the humility to embrace the unknown.

6.7 Design Takeaways: Embracing Incompleteness in DAO Governance

From Gödel to governance: Formal systems teach us that no rule-based architecture can be complete and self-sufficient. DAOs must be designed with this structural humility in mind.

1. Accept Ambiguity

Not all decisions can be pre-coded. Governance frameworks should leave space for deliberation and interpretation.

2. Enable Dissent

Healthy DAOs support structured disagreement. Dissent should be integrated, not suppressed.

3. Design for Memory

Beyond the ledger, DAOs need narrative continuity—rituals, storytelling, archives—to preserve collective identity and learning.

4. Avoid Closure

Resist the temptation of total codification. Incompleteness is not a bug but a safeguard against rigidity and epistemic overreach.

5. Curate, Don't Just Execute

Governance is not only a matter of automation, but of facilitation, care, and cultural curation.

References

De Filippi, P., & Wright, A. (2018). *Blockchain and the Law: The rule of code.* Harvard University Press.

Floridi, L. (2014). *The fourth revolution: How the infosphere is reshaping human reality.* Oxford University Press.

Gödel, K. (1931) Über formal unentscheidbare sätze der principia mathematica und verwandter systeme I. *Monatshefte Für Mathematik Und Physik*, *38*(1), 173–198.

Hilbert, D. (1928) Die Grundlagen der Mathematik. *Abhandlungen aus dem seminar der hamburgischen universität*, *6*(1), 65–85.

Hofstadter, D. R. (1979). *Gödel, Escher, Bach: An Eternal golden Braid.* Basic Books.

Lessig, L. (2006). *Code: Version 2.0.* Basic Books.

Reijers, W., & Coeckelbergh, M. (2018) The Blockchain as a narrative technology: investigating the social ontology and normative configurations of cryptocurrencies, *Philosophy & Technology, 31*(1), 103–130.

CHAPTER 7

Beyond Completeness: Designing DAO Governance for Ambiguity, Dissent, and Memory

7.1 Introduction: The Myth of Total Governance

If the previous chapter has shown us anything, it is that no system, no matter how elegantly formalized, rigorously encoded, or mathematically grounded, can ever fully contain its own logic. Gödel's (1931, 1962) incompleteness theorems taught us that any system capable of expressing arithmetic will inevitably encounter true statements it cannot prove.

In the context of decentralized governance, this insight is not merely philosophical: it is architectural. A decentralized autonomous organizations (DAOs) designed as a perfectly self-contained governance machine, expecting to anticipate and resolve all possible disputes, ambiguities, and edge cases, is not only unrealistic, but it is epistemologically impossible.

This chapter begins where Gödel leaves us: in the uncomfortable but fertile terrain of incompleteness. Rather than viewing this terrain as a flaw to be corrected, we treat it as a design condition to be embraced.

We ask: what kind of DAO emerges when we stop pretending that every outcome can be encoded in advance? What if ambiguity, dissent, and even contradiction are not bugs in the system, but essential dimensions of a resilient, living governance structure? (Fig. 7.1).

A. Cesaretti, *DAO Governance in Theory and Practice*,
https://doi.org/10.1007/978-3-032-09675-3_7

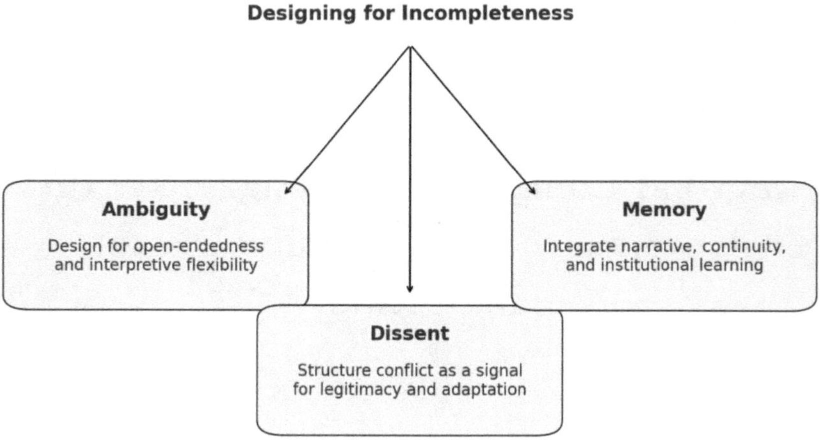

Fig. 7.1 Designing for incompleteness: three interdependent dimensions of DAO resilience. This diagram illustrates the three foundational pillars of resilient DAO governance explored in this chapter: Ambiguity, Dissent, and Memory. Rather than treating them as problems to be eliminated, these dimensions are reframed as necessary conditions for sustainable and adaptive decentralized systems. Together, they offer a framework for designing governance architectures that are incomplete by design—and stronger for it

7.1.1 DAO as the Dream of Full Formalization

From their inception, DAOs have embodied the ambition to transform human coordination into pure protocol. If traditional institutions rely on negotiation, interpretation, and trust, DAOs promise to replace ambiguity with code, discretion with determinism, and governance with automation.

In this view, the DAO becomes the dream of full formalization: an organization where all rules are explicit, all actions verifiable, and all outcomes computable. No backroom deals, no shifting norms, no hidden hierarchies, just a shared, transparent machine for making collective decisions.

But dreams of perfection often reveal their limits not in theory, but in practice. As DAOs scale, evolve, and encounter unforeseen contexts, they face the same paradox that Gödel revealed in mathematics: no system can fully contain the complexity of its own reality.

What if the DAO is not a machine that eliminates uncertainty, but a medium through which uncertainty becomes visible, navigable, and even generative?

7.1.2 *The Fallacy of "Complete Governance"*

The idea that a DAO can encode all its rules, resolve all conflicts, and govern itself without ambiguity is not just optimistic, it is structurally flawed. This is the fallacy of complete governance: the belief that protocol alone can substitute for politics, that smart contracts can preempt all disagreement, and that the right mechanism design can render institutions frictionless and final.

March and Olsen (1989) have already shown how even formal institutions rely on routines, identities, and symbolic practices that exceed codified logic. Treating governance as a purely procedural machine obscures the interpretive and cultural layers that shape actual outcomes.

But governance, at its core, is not about resolving choices that are already clear, it's about navigating what remains undecidable within the system. As Gödel demonstrated, no formal structure, no matter how intricate, can capture all truths about itself. In DAOs, this means there will always be edge cases, conflicting interpretations, contested priorities that no on-chain logic can fully resolve.

Pretending otherwise doesn't produce clarity; it produces brittleness. Systems built on the fantasy of completeness are not robust, they shatter when ambiguity inevitably arrives.

7.1.3 *Why Some Decisions Will Always Escape the Code*

A smart contract can enforce logic, but it cannot interpret context. It can verify inputs, but it cannot evaluate intentions. As long as DAOs operate in dynamic social, legal, and economic environments, they will inevitably face situations where the letter of the code is insufficient to capture the spirit of the problem.

These are not edge cases, they are the rule.

Decisions involving ethics, legitimacy, fairness, or contested interpretations of previous norms are fundamentally semantic and narrative, not just computational.

No matter how well-designed a voting system or incentive mechanism may be, there will always be moments when the community must ask: "What are we really deciding here?"

And that question cannot be answered on-chain. It requires discourse, memory, judgment, elements that live in the human layer, not the protocol layer.

In this sense, incompleteness is not a flaw in DAO design. It is a fact of political life.

7.2 Gödel, Incompleteness, and the Limits of Protocols

7.2.1 Brief Recap of Gödel's Theorems

In 1931, Austrian logician Kurt Gödel proved two theorems that changed the foundations of mathematics, and, by extension, any formal system that aspires to self-consistency and completeness. His results apply not only to number theory, but to all systems capable of expressing basic arithmetic and logical deduction.

The first incompleteness theorem states that in any consistent formal system that is powerful enough to express arithmetic, there exist true statements that cannot be proven within the system itself. In other words, no system can be both complete and consistent: if it avoids contradictions, it must necessarily leave some truths undecidable.

The second incompleteness theorem goes further: such a system cannot prove its own consistency from within. To verify that the system doesn't contradict itself, one must step outside the system, into a meta-system that, in turn, is also subject to incompleteness.

Gödel's theorems shattered the foundationalist dream of formal logic: that mathematics could be reduced to a complete, self-validating, mechanical procedure. But their relevance extends far beyond mathematics. Any system that encodes rules and seeks to govern itself autonomously, including a DAO, inherits these epistemological limits.

This insight resonates with critiques of technocratic rationality in political and organizational theory, where formal rule systems are often revealed as incomplete without interpretive frames and social embedding (Scott, 1998; Luhmann, 1995).

DAOs, like formal systems, are defined by internal rules and logic. They aspire to be self-enforcing and self-executing. Yet, Gödel tells us that there will always be decisions, exceptions, or conditions that the system cannot resolve without invoking principles external to its own rule set.

7.2.2 The Analogy with Smart Contracts and Voting Rules

Smart contracts are often described as "code as law." They are deterministic, verifiable, and, once deployed, operate autonomously based on predefined conditions. In this sense, they resemble formal systems: each contract encodes a bounded logical universe, complete with axioms (initial conditions), inference rules (conditional logic), and provable outputs (transactional consequences).

Voting rules, similarly, establish procedural mechanisms for decision-making: who can vote, how votes are counted, what thresholds apply, and what actions are triggered. These mechanisms aim to produce clarity and legitimacy through formalization.

But just like the systems Gödel studied, smart contracts and governance protocols have inherent epistemic boundaries. There will always be:

- Proposals that defy simple categorization,
- Disputes that hinge on intent rather than input,
- Or scenarios where following the rules produces results that violate the spirit of the community.

These aren't implementation bugs. They are logical consequences of the system's design.

Any rule-based framework powerful enough to govern a non-trivial organization will eventually encounter situations it cannot resolve from within.

Moreover, a protocol cannot prove its own legitimacy. It can define quorum, voting thresholds, and procedural validity, but it cannot justify why those rules should command allegiance, which requires external reference points: history, trust, and values.

In this light, smart contracts and voting rules are necessary but insufficient. They provide structure, but not meaning. They can enact, but not interpret.

And interpretation, narrative, memory, dissent, is where governance truly happens.

7.2.3 Governance Systems as Formal Languages: Where They Break

Every governance system, whether off-chain or on-chain, can be viewed as a formal language: a set of symbols (tokens, votes, proposals), syntactic rules (quorum thresholds, proposal structures), and semantics (intended effects, social meaning). Like any language, a governance system must balance expressiveness and decidability: the more situations it tries to encode, the more complex and fragile it becomes.

Smart contract-based DAOs often aim for high precision and low ambiguity, optimizing for machine execution, and minimizing interpretive friction. But this formalism comes at a cost: the system can only "see" and act upon what has been predefined in its ontology. Anything that falls outside its categories becomes unrecognizable, and therefore ungovernable.

This is where formal governance systems begin to break. The tension between syntactic closure and semantic openness has long been discussed in legal and institutional theory. As Ostrom (1990) and March and Olsen (1989) argue, robust governance emerges not from rigid codification, but from adaptable structures grounded in shared norms and evolving practices.

- A proposal that defies existing categories cannot be voted on.
- A vote that technically meets the threshold but violates shared norms may still pass—and fracture the community.
- A fork may become the only "logical" response to a semantic disagreement the protocol cannot represent.

These breakdowns mirror the points of failure in formal languages: ambiguity, incompleteness, and semantic drift. The DAO cannot collapse these contradictions within itself, because doing so would require a level of meta-interpretation that no formal system can provide.

In short, formal governance languages are closed under syntax but open under meaning.

And meaning is always context-dependent, evolving, and situated, never fully capturable by code

7.3 Quantum Governance: Plurality Without Collapse

7.3.1 Many-Worlds Interpretation and Forkable Universes

In the Many-Worlds Interpretation of quantum mechanics, every quantum event with multiple possible outcomes leads to a branching of the universe. There is no single, privileged reality: all outcomes happen, each in a separate and equally real world. Measurement does not collapse the wavefunction, it reveals a path through a multidimensional field of possibilities.

DAOs, by design or by accident, often operate under a similar logic. When a community faces an irreconcilable disagreement, whether political, technical, or ethical, it does not always converge toward resolution. Instead, it forks: a new contract, a new token, a new community. Like in quantum theory, the governance "universe" branches, and both paths continue to exist in parallel.

This view recasts DAO forks not as breakdowns, but as governance branching events. Each forked DAO preserves part of the original code and narrative, but carries forward a distinct interpretation of what the organization should become. Rather than assuming that governance should eliminate multiplicity, the Many-Worlds analogy invites us to embrace divergence as a generative feature.

7.3.2 Governance Branches and Contested Realities

Forks are not merely technical splits, they are ontological events. They mark the point at which a community stops agreeing not just on what to do, but on what the organization is. In this sense, forks are not deviations from consensus but manifestations of deep contestation about meaning, identity, and legitimacy.

Each governance branch becomes a kind of reality unto itself, with its own assumptions, values, and internal coherence. Token holders migrate. Narratives diverge. Even the memory of shared origin may begin to blur as each branch writes its own history.

This raises a crucial insight: *Governance is not only about decision-making. It is also about constructing a shared reality.*

DAOs, like quantum systems, do not always collapse into one clean outcome. Instead, they often produce coexisting truths, what one community sees as betrayal, another sees as emancipation; what one side calls an exploit, the other calls a correction.

These realities are not illusions. They are socially instantiated worlds, stabilized by code, discourse, and coordination. The governance protocol cannot adjudicate between them because it operates within only one branch at a time. It lacks a meta-perspective.

To design governance systems capable of surviving contestation, we must acknowledge that disagreement does not always require resolution. Sometimes, it simply requires containment, acknowledgment, and divergence.

7.3.3 Embracing Coexistence Over Consensus

The dominant ideal in governance design, both on-chain and off, is often consensus: the aspiration to unify divergent voices into a single, actionable decision. Yet in practice, especially within decentralized communities, consensus can become a tyrannical standard. It privileges closure over continuity, finality over flexibility.

In a truly distributed system, multiple interpretations, priorities, and value frameworks inevitably coexist. These do not always converge, and they do not need to. Attempting to resolve every disagreement through procedural convergence, voting, quorum, supermajority, risks flattening complexity into simplistic binaries.

What if we shifted our aim from consensus to coexistence?

Coexistence does not mean avoiding decision-making. It means designing governance processes that tolerate ambiguity, accommodate dissent, and preserve multiplicity without forcing premature closure.

This approach draws from the quantum metaphor: *in the Many-Worlds framework, each outcome continues independently. There is no collapse to a single truth, only divergent realities, each internally consistent, each valid from within its own frame.*

Similarly, a governance system built for coexistence allows different factions to experiment with divergent paths, while maintaining a substrate of dialogue, mutual observation, and reversible transitions. This resonates with Luhmann's (1995) insight that social systems are not maintained through consensus, but through the recursive processing of communication. Governance, from this view, becomes not a decision pipeline, but an evolving discourse system capable of holding plural narratives without collapsing them. In this way, governance becomes a living field of possibilities, rather than a mechanism for declaring one reality absolute.

7.3.4 Governance Without Finality

In blockchain infrastructure, finality is a technical goal: the point at which a transaction becomes irreversible and fully integrated into the chain's canonical history. But when this concept is extended to governance, it becomes deeply problematic.

Social decisions are rarely final. They are reinterpreted, revised, revoked, or replaced. New information emerges. Community norms evolve. What once seemed settled may later appear flawed. And yet, many DAO systems mimic the rigidity of transactional finality: once a vote passes, the outcome is encoded, immutable, and beyond contestation.

But governance is not a ledger, it is a conversation that unfolds over time.

Designing DAO governance as if it were a linear, irreversible process ignores the recursive and reflective nature of real-world coordination. Finality may be required for execution, but not for meaning. The decision might be enacted, but its legitimacy will continue to be debated, and that debate is part of governance, not noise external to it.

This is aligned with March and Olsen's (1989) critique of rationalist institutionalism: decisions are embedded in evolving interpretative frames and are always subject to retrospective meaning-making. Finality, in this context, is not a property of the system, but of the narrative that stabilizes it, temporarily.

A more resilient approach treats decisions as provisional commitments: valid in their context, subject to revision, and open to reinterpretation. Like a scientific hypothesis or a constitutional clause, a governance action gains authority not from its permanence, but from its capacity to remain meaningful in changing conditions.

This also implies that memory and traceability are more important than closure. What matters is not the definitive "yes or no," but how and why a community arrived at its conclusion, and what it remains willing to question.

7.3.5 Governance as an Open Wavefunction

If we accept that decentralized governance cannot be fully formalized, fully decided, or finally resolved, then we must also accept that governance is not a state, it is a wavefunction: a field of possibility, probability, and entangled perspectives.

Traditional models treat governance as a sequence of binary choices: yes or no, pass or fail, consensus or fork. But these models obscure the relational, iterative, and context-sensitive nature of decision-making. In practice, governance is always in motion: decisions reverberate, branches interact, meanings shift.

Just as in quantum systems, what we observe depends on how we observe it. A proposal's outcome is shaped not only by votes, but by framing, timing, narrative, and participation dynamics. The act of governance is never purely mechanical, it is performative.

The DAO, then, is not a machine for collapsing ambiguity.

It is a structure for cultivating and navigating ambiguity.

Designing for this means building protocols that are:

- Hospitable to uncertainty rather than allergic to it,
- Modular and reversible, rather than monolithic and final,
- Attuned to context, rather than abstracted from it.

In this sense, governance becomes not a search for closure, but a practice of sustaining coherence amid divergence, a kind of quantum stewardship, where the task is not to force one reality into dominance, but to hold open the field of possibility long enough for intelligence to emerge.

7.4 Designing for Incompleteness

7.4.1 Protocols as Frames, Not Prisons

One of the most common mistakes in DAO design is to treat the protocol as a totalizing structure: a machine meant to predefine all possible actions, anticipate all edge cases, and encode all necessary rules. This mindset assumes that ambiguity is a failure of specification, and that the solution lies in more code, more constraints, more completeness.

But a more resilient approach sees the protocol not as a prison, but as a frame, a scaffold for coordination that leaves space for interpretation, adaptation, and growth.

A good governance protocol is not a script to be followed line by line, but a canvas that invites meaningful participation.

This means designing with intentional incompleteness: recognizing that no rule set can foresee every scenario, and that true robustness lies in the system's capacity to adapt. Rather than trying to eliminate ambiguity, we can design boundaries within which ambiguity becomes generative.

Frames invite contributions, improvisation, contextual responses. They provide structure without foreclosure. This also means that protocols should:

- Allow for soft overrides (e.g., social signaling, off-chain deliberation),
- Include meta-governance mechanisms (rules to change the rules),
- And anticipate interpretive pluralism, not suppress it.

Ultimately, the DAO is not a closed system seeking internal perfection, but an open process shaped by human interaction. The protocol provides the tempo and tone, but the music comes from the community.

7.4.2 *Creating Space for Ambiguity (The Role of "Soft" Governance)*

Most governance frameworks treat ambiguity as a threat: something to be eliminated through precision, standardization, or automation. Yet in real communities, ambiguity is often where the richest meaning resides. As Geertz (1973) emphasized in his interpretive anthropology, ambiguity is not a defect of social systems but a site of cultural depth, where shared meanings are negotiated rather than prescribed. It is in the gray zones, between categories, across disciplines, beyond precedent, that creativity, empathy, and transformation take place.

In decentralized systems, ambiguity is not a design flaw, it is a source of adaptive capacity. A DAO that cannot tolerate ambiguity is a DAO that cannot evolve.

Creating space for ambiguity means:

- Recognizing that not all proposals fit cleanly into binary votes;
- Allowing for deliberation before codification;
- And designing mechanisms for pausing, rephrasing, or reframing decisions when the context is unclear.

It also means legitimizing ambiguity as part of the governance process. Sometimes the best governance action is not to decide, but to hold space for further exploration.

In art, ambiguity invites interpretation.

In science, it invites hypothesis.

In governance, it should invite participatory sense-making.

The goal is not to freeze ambiguity into premature clarity, but to build protocols that can coexist with uncertainty, without being paralyzed by it.

7.4.3 Accepting Dissent as Legitimate Signal, Not Noise

In many DAOs, dissent is treated as friction to be minimized, managed, or punished. Disagreement is pathologized as toxicity, fragmentation, or inefficiency. But in decentralized systems, where no one controls the narrative, dissent is not noise. It is a signal.

Healthy dissent reveals:

- Where assumptions are being contested,
- Where interests diverge,
- And where the existing structure may be insufficient to hold the complexity of the moment.

Rather than forcing convergence, resilient governance systems learn to listen to dissent as an early warning system. March and Olsen (1989) remind us that institutional learning often emerges from the margins, through anomalies, contestation, and deviation, rather than from consensus or routine.

A "no" is not always a rejection of the process, it may be a call to deepen it.

Designing for dissent means:

- Embedding minority protection mechanisms (like quorum checks, multi-round votes, or delegated escalation),
- Ensuring transparent archiving of objections, not just approvals,
- And fostering a culture where voicing dissent is a civic act, not a hostile move.

Just as in democratic theory, dissent is vital to legitimacy, in DAOs, it is essential to learning, self-correction, and renewal.

A governance process that cannot tolerate dissent is not robust, it is brittle, and eventually silent.

7.4.4 Case Study: Designing for Incompleteness in AgoraDAO

AgoraDAO is a decentralized platform for funding community-led research. Its members submit proposals, vote on grants, and oversee project milestones using a combination of smart contracts and off-chain deliberation.

Early on, the DAO implemented a minimalist governance protocol: one token, one vote; 51% majority rule; no moderation layer. It worked, until it didn't.

In its third funding round, a proposal emerged to finance a project on controversial bioethics research. The proposal technically met all the criteria: clear scope, transparent budget, and a credible team. But it sparked deep disagreement within the community, ethical, not procedural.

The vote passed narrowly. The losing side forked. Both DAOs survived, but trust, cohesion, and collective memory were fractured.

In the aftermath, AgoraDAO restructured its governance framework around the principles of intentional incompleteness:

- A deliberation period was added before voting, to allow proposals to evolve in response to critique.
- A new "Context Channel" was introduced: a narrative layer for annotating proposals with ethical, legal, or cultural concerns—not binding, but visible.
- Dissenting votes could now include structured objections, stored on IPFS and linked to the proposal archive, forming a long-term memory layer.

The DAO also created a "Pause & Reflect" mechanism, allowing any delegate group to temporarily halt a proposal for structured discussion.

Over time, AgoraDAO learned that what had seemed like inefficiency, ambiguity, dissent, delay, was actually governance in its most vital form: not the suppression of uncertainty, but its intelligent navigation.

In embracing its own incompleteness, AgoraDAO became more than a protocol.

It became a place for thinking together, before deciding.

7.4.5 *Designing With Incompleteness in Mind*

The greatest strength of a DAO is not its code, but its capacity to evolve alongside its community. And evolution requires space: space for ambiguity, for disagreement, for memory, for context that no smart contract can fully grasp.

Designing with incompleteness in mind means letting go of the fantasy of total control. It means shifting from precision to participation, from closure to coherence, from rules that decide everything to structures that support meaning-making over time.

This is not about abandoning rigor. It is about recognizing that rigor alone is not enough. The formal layer must be held within a broader ecology of narrative, values, and dialogue.

A DAO is not just a decision machine. It is a medium for collective sense-making under uncertainty.

And in that space of uncertainty, when encoded with care, humility, and openness, incompleteness becomes not a limitation, but a design feature for freedom, resilience, and collective intelligence.

7.5 Memory as a Governance Layer

7.5.1 *Why Archiving Matters in Decentralized Systems*

In decentralized governance, memory is often treated as incidental, an emergent byproduct of block explorers, Discord logs, or forum threads. But this neglects a crucial truth: without structured memory, there can be no continuity, no accountability, and no learning.

Unlike traditional institutions, which preserve memory through minutes, archives, and institutional culture, DAOs operate in ephemeral digital environments. Decisions are recorded immutably, but meaning is not. A vote exists on-chain, but the debate behind it may vanish in the noise of real-time discussion.

A DAO that forgets why it made a decision is no more resilient than one that never made it at all.

Archiving in decentralized systems is not merely historical, it is operational:

- It informs future decisions by recalling the rationale of past ones.
- It contextualizes dissent and tracks the evolution of contested norms.

- It enables interpretability over time, especially as tokenholders, delegates, and contributors rotate in and out.

Crucially, archiving is not just about storing data, it is about curating it: preserving the plurality of perspectives, surfacing key moments, and embedding semantic layers over raw transactions.

In a protocol that accepts incompleteness, memory is not a footnote. It is the connective tissue that allows meaning, legitimacy, and coherence to emerge across time.

7.5.2 *Narrative Continuity as a Form of Institutional Legitimacy*

In traditional institutions, legitimacy is built not only on procedures, but on stories: narratives that explain why decisions were made, how authority is exercised, and what values anchor collective identity. Constitutions, jurisprudence, and institutional rituals all serve as vehicles of narrative continuity.

In DAOs, where code replaces constitution and participation is often fluid, this narrative layer is frequently missing, or fragmented across disparate platforms. The result is that even perfectly valid decisions may feel arbitrary, disconnected, or illegible to new participants.

Without a coherent narrative, legitimacy becomes fragile, even if the protocol is sound.

As Geertz (1973) emphasized in his anthropological work, shared narratives are not decorative but constitutive of institutional coherence: they provide the symbolic frameworks through which actors interpret rules, roles, and collective identity.

Narrative continuity does not mean enforced consensus or a single version of history. It means maintaining a traceable, evolving story of how the DAO has changed, what it has wrestled with, and how it understands itself across time.

This continuity can take many forms:

- Public annotations attached to votes and proposals.
- Community-curated timelines of pivotal events.
- Reflective documentation of crises, forks, or shifts in mission.

Just as a legal precedent guides future rulings, past narrative anchors help future decisions find their place. They prevent the perpetual reinvention of purpose and allow new members to inherit not just rules, but meaning.

In short, a DAO without narrative continuity is a protocol without memory, technically operational, but politically incoherent.

7.5.3 *DAO as a Living Palimpsest: Governance Beyond the Vote*

A DAO is often reduced to its most visible mechanics: voting, funding proposals, and executing smart contracts. But beneath these formal acts lies a deeper, slower layer of governance, one composed of memory, reinterpretation, and narrative sedimentation.

This deeper layer is not linear. Like a palimpsest, a manuscript written and rewritten over time, a DAO accumulates traces: decisions amended, values debated, identities reframed.

Governance is not just what is decided, but how those decisions are remembered, recontextualized, and reinterpreted.

This perspective reveals why governance cannot be equated with voting alone. Votes are important, but they are moments in a longer arc. As March and Olsen (1989) argued, institutional meaning is not only encoded in formal decisions, but sedimented over time through routines, reinterpretations, and evolving logics of appropriateness. What gives them weight is their position in the collective narrative, the reasons behind them, the disputes they resolved or opened, and the precedents they created.

Designing a DAO as a living palimpsest means:

- Allowing governance history to remain editable in meaning, even if not in data.
- Encouraging meta-reflection: not just "what did we vote for?" but "what did that vote mean for us?"
- Building tools for layered memory: annotated archives, deliberation histories, cultural mappings.

Ultimately, a DAO built for longevity must be more than a machine of execution. It must be a medium of shared meaning-making over time, capable of integrating not just new code, but new interpretations of itself.

7.6 Design Proposals

7.6.1 Patterns and Anti-Patterns from Real DAOs

As the DAO ecosystem matures, it becomes increasingly clear that certain governance behaviors tend to repeat. Some contribute to resilience, learning, and long-term coherence. This reflects Ostrom's (1990) insight that robust institutions emerge not from rigid blueprints but from adaptive rules, nested structures, and context-sensitive practices developed through iterative experimentation. Others, though perhaps well-intentioned, often produce fragility, conflict, or stagnation.

Identifying "patterns and anti-patterns" allows designers to move beyond ideology and focus on what actually works, and what doesn't, in living decentralized systems.

Positive Patterns

- Iterative governance: DAOs that treat rules as provisional and open to revision (e.g., through meta-governance or "soft consensus" practices) tend to adapt better to unforeseen challenges.
- Layered participation: Effective DAOs often support multiple levels of engagement, from low-effort signaling (e.g., likes, delegations) to high-effort stewardship roles, allowing contributors to find their own pace and stake.
- Decision contextualization: Adding narrative layers, through forums, annotated proposals, or reflective documentation, helps ensure that decisions remain legible and legitimate over time.
- Constructive dissent channels: Mechanisms that surface dissent (like minority reports or structured objections) without forcing polarization enable nuanced governance without fragmentation.
- Stewardship and curation: Designating trusted roles for framing, interpreting, or synthesizing community input increases coherence without reintroducing hierarchy.

Recurrent Anti-Patterns

- Vote-only governance: Relying solely on token voting (with little deliberation or framing) tends to produce shallow decision-making, subject to manipulation and misinterpretation.

- Mechanism myopia: Overengineering incentives while neglecting narrative, culture, or meaning often leads to high transactional throughput but low institutional resilience.
- Hard finality without memory: Once-and-for-all decisions that lack archival context or reflective feedback loops can appear arbitrary or illegitimate, especially to newcomers.
- Suppression of dissent: Labeling disagreement as trolling or non-constructive undermines participation and accelerates silent exits or forks.
- Constant redesign without learning: DAOs that repeatedly pivot or restructure without internalizing past mistakes often repeat them, failing not from lack of change, but from lack of memory.

Governance design is not about importing a perfect model, it's about recognizing recurring traps, nurturing effective patterns, and allowing space for divergence without collapse.

7.6.2 Templates for "Incomplete" DAO Architecture

The most resilient DAOs are not those that seek to eliminate ambiguity, but those that create structured spaces for ambiguity to be negotiated, remembered, and reinterpreted. Designing for incompleteness requires moving beyond rigid blueprints toward modular, adaptive, and narratively-aware architectures.

Here are three conceptual templates that illustrate this shift.

1. Layered Governance Stack

A governance architecture that separates functions by layer, allowing each to evolve semi-independently:

- Execution layer: Smart contracts and automated processes.
- Deliberation layer: Forums, annotations, and contextual archives.
- Meta-governance layer: Rules for proposing, modifying, or suspending procedures.
- Memory layer: Archival tools, dissent logs, narrative timelines.

Each layer answers a different question: What are we doing? Why are we doing it? How can we change the process? What have we learned?

2. Fork-Ready Protocols

Instead of avoiding forks at all costs, this model embraces forking as a native function, not as failure, but as divergence management.

Features include:

- Pre-fork dialogue channels to clarify positions and expectations.
- Soft forking tools that allow experimentation without full exit (e.g., subDAOs, parallel tracks).
- Post-fork memory bridges: Annotated records of divergence, shared ancestry trees, or interoperable registries.

In this architecture, legitimacy does not come from unity, but from transparent divergence.

3. Embedded Roles for Narrative and Reflection

A DAO designed around the principle of curated memory and ongoing interpretation integrates roles beyond developers and voters:

- Stewards who maintain coherence across layers and cycles.
- Curators who archive, annotate, and contextualize decisions.
- Narrative facilitators who help frame conflicts, transitions, and shared meaning.

These roles are not authorities, they are interpreters of a living system, enabling memory to remain active rather than inert.

In an incomplete architecture, structure does not guarantee certainty, it invites continuous meaning-making.

These templates are not prescriptive. They are design invitations, starting points for imagining DAOs that are not brittle machines of decision, but resilient environments for ongoing collective intelligence.

In traditional organizations, structure is upheld by roles like managers, administrators, or legal counsel. March and Olsen (1989) have emphasized that institutional roles do more than execute functions, they also sustain collective meaning, frame decision contexts, and reproduce legitimacy over time. In DAOs, where formal authority is minimized, the absence of these coordinating functions can produce drift, fragmentation, or paralysis. But this vacuum is not inevitable. It can be filled by new kinds of roles, ones aligned with modularity, plurality, and narrative continuity.

Beyond developers and voters, DAOs require human roles that interpret, connect, and sustain meaning across time.

These roles do not command, they curate, connect, and contextualize. As Scott (1998) reminds us, attempts to render institutions fully "legible" often erase the informal, narrative, and tacit practices that sustain real-world governance. These interpretive roles help retain that richness.

1. Stewards

Stewards act as continuity anchors. They help maintain procedural coherence, ensure that evolving governance tools remain intelligible, and often serve as custodians of institutional memory.

Responsibilities may include:

- Documenting changes in rules or frameworks.
- Mediating transitions or upgrades.
- Holding space during uncertainty or ambiguity.

Good stewards are not rule enforcers, they are ecosystem gardeners.

2. Curators

Curators manage the DAO's epistemic infrastructure: they archive discussions, tag themes, compile dissent, and trace the genealogy of key decisions. In doing so, they help prevent institutional amnesia.

Key functions:

- Making deliberation legible across time.
- Preserving alternative viewpoints and interpretations.
- Surfacing relevant precedent when new proposals arise.

Curation is memory design.

3. Narrative Facilitators

These are the sense-makers of the DAO. When conflicts emerge, when proposals divide the community, or when meaning begins to fracture, narrative facilitators help reframe the problem, clarify stakes, and weave coherence across divergent views.

They do not dictate outcomes. They hold the space where meaning can emerge.

Without these roles, governance collapses into procedure.

With them, governance becomes a living discourse.

DAOs that embrace these functions, even informally, tend to exhibit higher resilience, stronger community bonds, and deeper institutional learning.

Designing for incompleteness does not mean abandoning structure.

It means investing in the right kind of structure: one that listens, remembers, and evolves.

7.7 Conclusion: Incompleteness as Strength

7.7.1 *Letting Go of the Fantasy of Perfect Consensus*

Consensus is often framed as the holy grail of decentralized governance. But in reality, the pursuit of perfect consensus can become a trap: it delays action, suppresses dissent, and masks underlying complexity.

Worse, it generates the illusion that if we just design the right voting system or incentive mechanism, we can finally eliminate conflict, ambiguity, and fragmentation.

But governance is not a puzzle to be solved. It is a conversation to be sustained.

Letting go of the fantasy of perfect consensus does not mean embracing chaos. It means recognizing that plurality is a feature, not a bug. It means designing systems that are not afraid of disagreement, divergence, or even temporary incoherence.

A DAO that welcomes divergence becomes more than a decision engine, it becomes a site of collective inquiry.

And in that space of inquiry, legitimacy is no longer tied to unanimity. It emerges from transparency, continuity, and trust in the process, even when outcomes are contested.

This view resonates with Ostrom's (1990) insight that enduring governance systems rely not on formal unanimity, but on shared norms, mutual monitoring, and trust built through repeated interactions.

7.7.2 *Designing for Evolution, Not Enforcement*

Traditional governance systems are often built around the logic of enforcement: rules are established, monitored, and punished when broken. But in decentralized contexts, where authority is diffuse, values are dynamic, and participation is fluid, enforcement has diminishing returns.

A DAO is not a fortress to be defended. It is an organism to be nurtured.

Designing for evolution means creating governance structures that can:

- Adapt to emergent contexts without overhauling the entire system.
- Learn from exceptions, rather than suppress them.
- Embrace revision and iteration as signs of maturity, not weakness.

This requires building mechanisms not only for decision-making, but for:

- Feedback loops that carry insight from the edge back to the core.
- Meta-governance that enables the system to reflect on itself.
- Cultural protocols that reinforce values even when the code cannot.

Enforcement assumes finality. Evolution assumes incompleteness, and turns it into a condition for learning.

The goal is not to get it right once, but to stay right enough, long enough, by evolving with integrity. This aligns with March and Olsen's (1989) argument that institutions are not static arrangements but evolving orders, shaped by learning, reinterpretation, and cultural adaptation.

7.7.3 *From Command to Context: A New Language for DAO Governance*

The language of traditional governance is rooted in command: authority, control, compliance. Even in DAOs, this language persists, translated into votes, smart contracts, enforcement mechanisms. But as Scott (1998) reminds us, overly rigid systems that ignore local context and lived experience often fail not due to lack of control, but because they fail to see. But as we've seen, decentralization requires a different grammar: one grounded not in control, but in context.

When rules fail, it's not because they are disobeyed. It's because they're disconnected, from lived experience, shared values, and collective understanding.

Governance through context means:

- Designing rules that invite interpretation, not just execution.
- Prioritizing narrative coherence over procedural completeness.
- Embedding meaning and memory into every layer of decision-making.

This shift is not cosmetic, it is structural.

It asks us to stop thinking of DAOs as machines for compliance and start seeing them as ecosystems for sense-making. This echoes the shift described by March and Olsen (1989), who distinguish between the logic of consequence and the logic of appropriateness, emphasizing that governance is as much about meaning and identity as about outcomes.

- From "How do we enforce this rule?" to "What is the shared story that makes this rule matter?"
- From "How do we eliminate ambiguity?" to "How do we navigate and remember it together?"

In this light, incompleteness is not a governance failure. It is the terrain on which governance becomes alive.

This shift sets the stage for understanding DAOs not just as narrative spaces, but as complex adaptive systems (CAS), dynamic ecologies of interaction, memory, and institutional learning, as explored in Chap. 9.

The principles of embracing incompleteness and narrative governance explored here will inform the more detailed institutional designs and metrics discussed in Chap. 9 and beyond.

As we move from narrative frameworks to dynamic institutional structures, Chap. 9 examines how DAOs function as CAS, fluid, decentralized ecosystems that evolve through feedback, emergence, and multi-agent interaction.

7.8 Design Takeaways: Governance Beyond Completeness

Designing DAOs for ambiguity, dissent, and memory means accepting that not all problems are solvable in advance. The following principles offer guidance for building decentralized institutions that remain legitimate, adaptive, and resilient under uncertainty.

1. Design for Ambiguity

Codified rules should be complemented by flexible spaces for interpretation and deliberation.

2. Structure Dissent

Disagreement is not noise but signal. Create governance layers where dissent can be expressed, processed, and re-integrated.

3. Institutionalize Memory

DAOs need collective memory, rituals, archives, and narratives, to preserve meaning and support continuity across time and change.

4. Use Forks as Ritual, Not Only Rupture

Forking can be structured to maintain dialogue and shared memory, not just exit and division.

5. Balance Formality with Narrative

Governance frameworks should be legible in code, but meaningful in culture. Narrative coherence is as important as procedural transparency.

References

Geertz, C. (1973). *The interpretation of cultures.* Basic Books.

Gödel, K. (1931). Über formal unentscheidbare Sätze der Principia Mathematica und verwandter Systeme I. *Monatshefte Für Mathematik Und Physik, 38*, 173–198.

Gödel, K. (1962). *On formally undecidable propositions of principia mathematica and related systems.* Dover Publications.

Luhmann, N. (1995). *Social systems.* Stanford University Press.

March, J. G., & Olsen, J. P. (1989). *Rediscovering institutions: The organizational basis of politics.* Free Press.

Ostrom, E. (1990). *Governing the commons: The evolution of institutions for collective action.* Cambridge University Press.

Scott, J. C. (1998). *Seeing like a state: How certain schemes to improve the human condition have failed.* Yale University Press.

CHAPTER 8

DAOs as Complex Adaptive Systems: Governance Under Conditions of Decentralized Complexity

8.1 Introduction

Traditional models of governance and organizational design often rest on the assumption that institutions function as static systems governed by fixed rules, predictable cause-effect relationships, and linear decision-making pathways. Such deterministic models assume that, once protocols and procedures are defined, institutional behavior will follow predictable and controllable trajectories.

Yet in DAOs, governance emerges from fluid and interdependent interactions among participants, smart contracts, narratives, and external environments, defying any fixed blueprint.

While DAOs are implemented through smart contracts and deterministic code, their actual functioning emerges from complex interactions among autonomous participants, shifting social dynamics, market signals, and external regulatory environments. DAOs are not static protocols but evolving ecosystems in which governance outcomes are shaped by factors far beyond the lines of code.

These observations demand a shift from Newtonian thinking, which seeks precision, stability, and predictability, toward a paradigm grounded in complex adaptive systems (CAS) theory. In CAS, systems are composed of numerous interacting agents whose local interactions give rise to

A. Cesaretti, *DAO Governance in Theory and Practice*,
https://doi.org/10.1007/978-3-032-09675-3_8

emergent global patterns that cannot be deduced purely from the system's rules. Such systems exhibit:

- Emergence, where collective behaviors arise unpredictably from simple interactions.
- Non-linearity, where small inputs can lead to disproportionately large outcomes.
- Adaptivity, enabling systems to change structure and function in response to environmental pressures.

These properties are not abstract concepts. They map directly onto the behavior of DAOs, which exhibit unpredictable decision dynamics, amplification of small signals, and the capacity to evolve governance structures through iterative experimentation.

Applied to DAOs, this perspective reveals that governance processes:

- are subject to rapid shifts due to cascading effects of social or economic signals,
- depend on informal norms and narratives alongside formal voting mechanisms,
- evolve over time as participants learn, adapt, and reorganize collective decision-making structures.

This chapter aims to:

- Reframe DAOs as CAS, highlighting their dynamic, evolving nature.
- Introduce key operational concepts such as emergence, feedback loops, governance fitness landscapes, and phase transitions.
- Provide a foundation for designing DAO governance systems capable of embracing complexity rather than seeking to suppress it.

Ultimately, embracing a complexity-informed perspective allows us to transcend rigid protocol thinking and reimagine DAO governance as a dynamic, learning-oriented process, one that thrives not by resisting uncertainty, but by integrating it as a core condition of institutional life.

8.2 Fundamentals of Complexity in Institutional Systems

8.2.1 *What is a Complex Adaptive System (CAS)?*

A CAS is a decentralized network of interacting agents, individuals, organizations, or processes, whose local interactions give rise to emergent global patterns that cannot be reduced to formal rules or initial conditions. (Holland, 1992), (Gell-Mann, 1994), and (Waldrop, 1992). CAS are characterized by:

- Emergence: Novel structures and behaviors arise from interactions among agents without central coordination. For instance, ant colonies build intricate nests without a master blueprint, driven by local chemical signals.
- Non-linearity: Small changes in inputs can produce disproportionately large effects. A minor shift in an agent's behavior may cascade into system-wide transformations.
- Adaptivity: Agents continuously adjust their strategies in response to feedback from the environment or from other agents, leading the system to evolve over time.
- Distributed control: No single agent has complete oversight of the system. Instead, order emerges from decentralized interactions and adaptive processes.
- Feedback loops: Both positive feedback (which amplifies trends) and negative feedback (which stabilizes the system) shape the system's evolution.

Examples of CAS abound across disciplines: ecosystems, markets, urban environments, neural networks, and social communities all exhibit behaviors that emerge from countless micro-interactions rather than centralized command structures. As Scott (2008) and Ostrom (1990) note, even institutions, often thought of as rigid rule systems, can evolve as adaptive complexes when shaped by feedback, shared narratives, and contextual negotiation.

This framing draws from foundational work in complexity theory and institutional analysis. Holland (1992) introduced CAS as systems capable of decentralized adaptation; Gell-Mann (1994) emphasized the interplay between simplicity and emergence, while Waldrop (1992) explored how complexity arises at the edge of order and chaos. In governance studies, Ostrom (1990) illustrated how self-organizing institutions operate under conditions of distributed control and local adaptation, features mirrored in many DAO ecosystems.

8.2.2 Relevance to Governance

When applied to governance, this conceptual framework reveals its full explanatory power. Whether in hierarchical institutions or decentralized networks like DAOs, governance systems exhibit hallmark features of CAS. Governance systems are not static rulebooks but living architectures shaped by evolving interactions among participants, contextual signals, and institutional memory.

Whether centralized or decentralized, they reflect the adaptive, emergent qualities of CAS, as noted in the institutionalist traditions of March and Olsen (1984) and Ostrom (1990)

In governance contexts:

- Emergent properties arise from local decisions. In DAOs, for example, collective sentiment and informal narratives can drive voting outcomes even when the formal rules remain unchanged.
- Non-linear effects manifest when seemingly minor events—like a single delegate's vote or a viral social media post—trigger large-scale changes in policy or organizational direction.
- Adaptivity becomes crucial as governance systems must adjust to external shocks, regulatory shifts, or technological developments without losing coherence or legitimacy.
- Distributed decision-making reflects the lack of a single, controlling authority in many DAOs. Coordination arises through protocols, social norms, and adaptive negotiation among participants.
- Feedback loops influence institutional learning. Successful governance mechanisms may become reinforced, while failed experiments prompt structural reforms.

Traditional models of governance often rely on static frameworks and deterministic assumptions, expecting predictable cause-and-effect relationships. However, the empirical reality, particularly in DAOs, reveals governance as a complex, adaptive phenomenon where patterns of coordination, conflict, and innovation continuously evolve.

Scott's (2008) tripartite model of institutions, as composed of regulative, normative, and cultural-cognitive elements, underscores how governance transcends formal procedures, relying equally on shared meanings and informal coordination, both central to DAO functioning.

Understanding DAOs as CAS provides critical insights for institutional design:

- It challenges the notion that formal rules alone can fully determine outcomes.
- It emphasizes the importance of observing emergent patterns rather than imposing rigid top-down control.
- It encourages the development of governance architectures capable of absorbing uncertainty and adapting to change, rather than merely enforcing static rules.

Recognizing governance as a CAS is not just an academic exercise; it has profound practical implications for how we build resilient, adaptive institutions in a decentralized world.

This view aligns with March and Olsen's (1984) conception of governance as a dynamic interplay of formal structures and informal practices, where legitimacy and adaptation emerge through iterative negotiation. It also resonates with Scott's (2008) multi-level model of institutions, which includes regulative, normative, and cultural-cognitive pillars—each of which finds expression in DAO ecosystems through protocol rules, community norms, and shared narratives.

The following illustration conceptualizes DAO governance as a fitness landscape, where different governance architectures correspond to adaptive peaks or fragile valleys within a dynamic terrain. Navigating this landscape requires institutional learning, experimentation, and a capacity for procedural evolution. This recognition prepares us to reframe DAO governance not as a linear process, but as adaptive navigation across a rugged fitness landscape, where institutional learning, experimentation, and contextual alignment determine survival and success (Fig. 8.1)

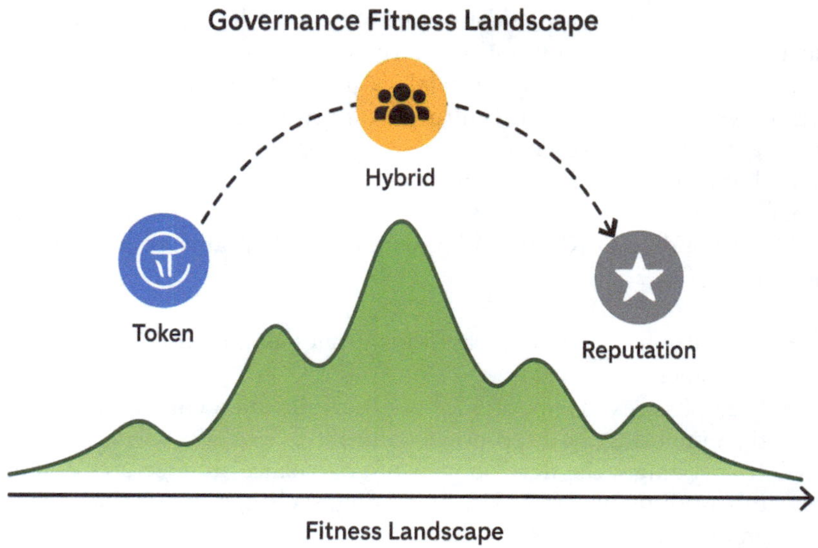

Fig. 8.1 DAO Governance Fitness Landscape. A conceptual illustration of the governance fitness landscape. Each peak represents a potentially resilient governance configuration; valleys indicate fragile or unsustainable structures. DAO evolution involves moving across this terrain through experimentation, adaptation, and institutional learning

8.3 Emergence and Non-linear Dynamics in DAO Governance

8.3.1 Patterns of Emergent Behavior in DAO Governance

One of the defining features of CAS is emergence: the spontaneous appearance of new structures, norms, or collective behaviors that are not explicitly coded into the system's formal rules but arise from distributed interactions. In DAOs, such emergent dynamics shape governance trajectories in ways that often defy initial protocol expectations, revealing patterns of adaptation, influence, and innovation that evolve from the interactions of autonomous participants.

Several key patterns of emergence can be observed in DAO governance:

Spontaneous Social Norms
Although DAOs operate through explicit smart contracts, many governance behaviors are driven by informal norms that develop over time. For instance, communities may adopt unwritten expectations about how delegates should disclose conflicts of interest, or how much discussion time should precede a formal vote. These norms emerge from repeated interactions rather than from protocol design.

Latent Coordination (Spontaneous Alignment of Votes)
DAO participants frequently align their votes without explicit coordination. This latent coordination arises through shared narratives, common incentives, or reputational cues. For example, in Uniswap governance, influential posts on forums can signal a "community direction," prompting independent actors to vote similarly, even without direct communication.

Memetics and Narrative Shaping
Memes, slogans, and symbolic language wield significant power in DAOs. These narrative units function as cultural attractors (Gell-Mann, 1994), guiding participant sentiment and influencing governance choices beyond rational deliberation. Memes such as "Exit to Community" or "WAGMI" (We're All Gonna Make It) do not merely communicate information, they encode shared values, mobilize emotions, and foster identity alignment. In Curve DAO, the concept of "Curve Wars" became a memetic framing of competitive liquidity incentives, fundamentally shaping governance behavior, coalition formation, and external strategic positioning.

This dynamic recalls the insights of Scott (2008) and Tilly (2005), who stress the role of narratives and symbolic repertoires in the construction of institutional legitimacy and collective coordination. Within DAO ecosystems, memes act as both communication shortcuts and governance vectors, enabling spontaneous alignment without formal agreements.

These emergent phenomena also mirror what Holland (1992) describes as the "rules of emergence" in adaptive systems, where macro-level patterns result from simple micro-level interactions without centralized control. Understanding these dynamics is critical for DAO resilience.

These patterns underscore that governance in DAOs is not merely about rules enforced by code, but about emergent social dynamics. Recognizing and understanding these dynamics is critical for designing resilient and adaptive governance systems.

8.3.2 Non-linear Effects

In DAOs, as in other complex systems, governance outcomes often exhibit non-linear dynamics, situations where small inputs or seemingly minor events produce disproportionately large effects. Such phenomena challenge deterministic models of governance, highlighting the unpredictable and sometimes volatile nature of decentralized systems.

Key examples of non-linearity in DAO governance include:

Minor Changes Leading to Major Governance Shifts
A slight change in narrative framing or a single influential endorsement can reverse the anticipated outcome of a governance vote. For example, in MakerDAO, an initially unpopular proposal gained momentum after a respected delegate published an analysis shifting community perception.

Informational Cascades
When prominent figures in a DAO express opinion, other participants may rapidly align with those views, not necessarily because of independent agreement, but due to social proof. In Yearn Finance, public endorsements by high-profile community members have repeatedly triggered sudden shifts in voting trends, leading to outcomes that would not have been predicted purely from prior token distributions.

Exponential Feedback Loops
DAOs often experience complex feedback cycles in which governance decisions affect token prices, which in turn alter participant composition and future decision-making dynamics. This recursive interplay generates exponential feedback loops, where small inputs can trigger large, system-wide effects. For example:

- A governance vote approving a new protocol feature may signal innovation, driving token price increases.
- Rising prices attract new participants or "whales" seeking influence or profit.
- The entrance of these actors shifts voting power and sentiment, producing governance outcomes that further affect token value and protocol direction.

These dynamics mirror what complexity theorists describe as "reflexive loops" (March & Olsen, 1984; Callon, 1998), where actions reshape the environment that, in turn, alters the conditions for future action. In DAO ecosystems, such loops are not only economic but narrative and reputational, often accelerating transitions between governance equilibria.

These non-linear effects imply that DAO governance cannot be reliably modeled as a static, linear process. Instead, governance must be approached as a dynamic, probabilistic phenomenon where emergent patterns and tipping points play decisive roles.

Understanding these non-linearities is essential for:

- anticipating potential governance crises,
- designing safeguards against manipulative cascades,
- and building protocols capable of absorbing shocks without catastrophic collapse.

Such dynamics are well-documented in complexity science, where small perturbations in interconnected systems can trigger critical transitions (Waldrop, 1992). These "butterfly effects" highlight the necessity for DAO governance to incorporate real-time monitoring and adaptive safeguards.

These observations reinforce the necessity of governance designs that anticipate unpredictability, rather than attempting to eliminate it. DAO systems must include buffers, adaptable components, and iterative learning mechanisms, acknowledging that non-linearity is a feature, not a bug, of decentralized coordination. As Waldrop (1992) suggests in his seminal study of complexity, the most robust systems are not those that prevent surprises, but those that evolve through them.

8.4 Feedback Loops and Institutional Learning

8.4.1 Types of Feedback in DAOs

Feedback loops are core features of CAS, shaping how DAOs evolve, self-regulate, and learn over time. Rather than being predesigned or centrally enforced, feedback in decentralized governance arises organically from ongoing interactions, shifting incentives, and institutional responses. As Holland (1992) observed, such loops enable adaptive behavior: they amplify successful strategies and dampen harmful ones through recursive adjustment. Feedback can either amplify change (positive feedback) or stabilize systems against volatility (negative feedback). In DAOs, these dynamics often interweave, producing governance behaviors that are highly sensitive to internal and external signals.

8.4.1.1 Positive Feedback: Reinforcing Loops

Positive feedback loops amplify trends and behaviors, often triggering rapid transformations in governance dynamics. In DAOs, such loops emerge when signals—whether from votes, narratives, or incentives—gain momentum through social reinforcement:

- Whale signaling: When large token holders take visible positions, they do more than cast votes, they shape expectations. In protocols like Yearn, a whale's endorsement can catalyze alignment, converting marginal support into landslides.
- Narrative contagion: Memes like "Curve Wars" don't just describe events—they create them. By framing governance as a contest for liquidity control, such narratives attract participation and escalate engagement, reinforcing themselves with each iteration.

8.4.1.2 Negative Feedback: Stabilizing Mechanisms

Negative feedback mechanisms serve to stabilize DAO governance by dampening volatility and curbing abrupt shifts. Examples include:

- Quorum thresholds, which block low-participation proposals and mitigate the influence of small, coordinated minorities.
- Timelocks, which delay execution after a vote, giving the community a buffer period to contest or reassess controversial outcomes.

These mechanisms act as institutional "brakes," fostering deliberation and preventing governance from overreacting to transient shocks or manipulation.

This stabilizing role of negative feedback echoes Holland's (1992) foundational work on CAS, where negative loops act to preserve systemic coherence under changing conditions.

8.4.1.3 Cross-Domain Feedback

Cross-domain feedback loops are particularly salient in DAO governance, where social, economic, and technological signals interact across boundaries. A decision taken in governance may influence token markets, which then reshape community sentiment and future votes.

For instance:

- A proposal to integrate a new protocol may boost token price.
- Rising prices attract new stakeholders with distinct governance preferences.
- These new actors shift the political equilibrium, influencing future proposals.

This recursive dynamic illustrates the co-evolution of institutional behavior and environmental conditions, a hallmark of complex systems as described by March and Olsen (1984) and Waldrop (1992). In DAOs, boundaries between social discourse, technical infrastructure, and economic behavior are porous, amplifying the entanglement between internal governance and external environments.

Such feedback loops create governance ecosystems where social, economic, and technological domains are deeply intertwined.

8.4.2 Institutional Memory

In CAS, institutional memory is essential for resilience and long-term coherence. It enables DAOs to learn from past experiences, preserve contextual understanding, and avoid repeating systemic failures.

In practice, DAOs cultivate memory through:

- Governance archives: Historical records of proposals, votes, delegate rationales, and discussions are crucial for continuity. For example, MakerDAO's governance portal maintains detailed archives that inform ongoing decisions and reduce epistemic drift.
- Narrative memory: Collective events are encoded in shared language and metaphors. Incidents like "Black Thursday" or the "Curve Wars" become reference points shaping governance behavior and risk perception.

Yet memory is not merely technical. Following Scott's (2008) distinction between regulative, normative, and cultural-cognitive elements, memory in DAOs functions across symbolic, procedural, and social registers. Similarly, Ostrom (1990) and March and Olsen (1984) highlight how institutions evolve through feedback-informed practices that embed past experiences into current behavior.

However, challenges persist:

- Information may be scattered across forums, chats, and dashboards.
- Newcomers often lack historical context, leading to redundant debates or poor decision-making.

Building resilient institutional memory requires intentional design:

- Curation tools to structure archives and highlight critical lessons.
- Onboarding pathways that transmit key historical narratives and norms.
- Reflexive mechanisms (e.g., periodic retrospectives or post-mortems) to transform experience into actionable learning.

As in any CAS, memory is not static record-keeping, but an active substrate for institutional evolution.

8.4.3 Learning Mechanisms

For DAOs to remain viable in volatile environments, they must function as learning institutions, continuously adjusting their governance structures and norms in response to internal feedback and external shocks.

As Holland (1992) notes, adaptive systems evolve by learning from experience and modifying local rules. In governance contexts, this means that institutional reflexivity—an organization's capacity to observe and change its own behavior—is vital.

DAOs Typically Embed Learning Through Three Core Mechanisms.

1. Meta-Governance

Meta-governance refers to the capacity of a system to modify its own rules. In DAOs, this takes the form of:

- Proposals that update voting thresholds, delegate structures, or incentive mechanisms.
- Procedural self-modification tools, such as those implemented in Aragon or Optimism, which allow the protocol to evolve without requiring a hard fork.

This aligns with March & Olsen's (1984) conception of governance as iterative rule renegotiation.

2. Dynamic Parameters

Rather than relying on fixed governance settings, DAOs often deploy dynamic mechanisms that adapt in real time:

- Variable quorum requirements, based on participation levels or proposal risk.
- Reputation-based voting weights, adjusting influence according to contribution history or contextual expertise.

These mechanisms embody the principle of feedback adaptation—systems that recalibrate internal parameters based on environmental signals.

3. Reflexive Processes

Reflexivity is the ability to extract insight from past actions. DAOs operationalize this through:

- Post-mortems following failed proposals, attacks, or crises (e.g., MakerDAO's response to Black Thursday).
- Conflict analysis and governance retrospectives to identify gaps in rules or cultural misalignments.
- Narrative reconstruction, where the community reinterprets past events to inform future strategies.

As Ostrom (1990) emphasizes, robust institutions are not static rulebooks but co-produced arrangements shaped by experimentation, contextual learning, and collective memory.

In sum, learning mechanisms transform DAOs from fragile automata into resilient, co-evolving systems capable of sustaining legitimacy under uncertainty.

8.5 Foundations of Governance Fitness Landscapes

8.5.1 Conceptual Foundations

The concept of a fitness landscape, originally developed in evolutionary biology, provides a powerful metaphor for understanding governance design in DAOs. In biology, fitness landscapes describe how different genetic combinations yield varying levels of reproductive success, with adaptive peaks representing configurations of high fitness and valleys indicating fragile or maladaptive arrangements.

This metaphor has been extended to organizational and institutional design by scholars such as Axelrod and Cohen (2000) and Holland (1992). Applied to DAOs, it invites us to visualize governance structures as dynamic configurations that must adapt to shifting internal and external conditions to maintain viability.

In institutional terms, "fitness" is not a single variable but a multi-dimensional construct encompassing:

- Robustness: The ability to withstand shocks and preserve operational continuity.
- Resilience: The capacity to reorganize in response to disruption without losing identity.
- Legitimacy: Perceived fairness, inclusiveness, and procedural transparency.
- Efficiency: The ability to make timely and cost-effective decisions.

A governance system may excel in one area (e.g., efficiency) while underperforming in another (e.g., legitimacy), placing it on a local optimum that is suboptimal in the broader landscape.

These dimensions reflect what March and Olsen (1984) describe as the tension between institutional coherence and adaptability, and what Ostrom (1990) frames as the challenge of sustaining collective action under conditions of limited information and distributed authority.

Viewing DAOs through the lens of the fitness landscape emphasizes the importance of:

- Experimentation and learning,
- Recognition of path dependencies,
- The possibility of institutional lock-in or maladaptation.

It also provides a conceptual bridge between technical protocol design and institutional theory: governance is no longer a question of optimizing one variable (like voter participation or token alignment) but of navigating a rugged terrain of interdependent trade-offs under uncertainty

8.5.2 Fitness Peaks and Valleys

Within the governance fitness landscape, certain configurations emerge as fitness peaks—institutional forms that perform well across multiple dimensions such as robustness, legitimacy, and efficiency. Others fall into fitness valleys, where governance mechanisms produce fragility, disengagement, or systemic risk.

Fitness Peaks are achieved when:

- Delegation structures balance responsiveness and representation.
- Reputation mechanisms incentivize thoughtful participation.
- Dispute resolution is effective without centralizing authority.

For instance, MakerDAO's delegate system, by combining token-weighted voting with reputational scrutiny, has achieved partial success in scaling governance while retaining community legitimacy, a local peak under its current constraints.

In contrast, Fitness Valleys arise when:

- Governance becomes dominated by whales, undermining legitimacy.
- Excessive procedural rigidity blocks adaptation.
- Fragmented communities fail to reach quorum or consensus.

The concept of path dependence is crucial here: once a DAO adopts a particular structure, institutional inertia and stakeholder expectations may entrench it, even if better alternatives exist (March & Olsen, 1984).

Moving to a higher-fitness configuration may require temporary destabilization, passing through a valley of lower performance or legitimacy.

In such cases, adaptive traps can occur, systems that are locally stable but globally suboptimal. Escaping them requires intentional mechanisms for meta-governance, experimentation, or even structural disruption (e.g., protocol forks).

As Taleb (2012) notes in his work on antifragility, systems that evolve successfully are those that do not avoid stress altogether, but learn how to use it to reach more resilient configurations. For DAOs, this may involve:

- Accepting short-term turbulence to pursue longer-term governance improvement.
- Designing transition pathways that reduce exit costs or reputational fragmentation.

Forks, in this light, represent radical evolutionary leaps across the landscape. While costly, they may be the only way to escape deep valleys or to pursue fundamentally different governance philosophies.

8.5.3 Navigating the Landscape

Successfully navigating the governance fitness landscape requires an intentional balance between exploration (pursuing novel governance models) and exploitation (refining existing strengths). As March (1991) argues, effective organizations alternate between these modes to adapt without losing coherence.

In DAO contexts, this means combining modifiability, experimentation, and resilience mechanisms that permit evolution without collapse.

8.5.3.1 Modifiable Parameters

Dynamic governance settings such as:

- Adjustable quorum thresholds,
- Voting weights responsive to reputation or past engagement,
- Execution timelocks and grace periods

Help DAOs fine-tune their institutional settings. This allows incremental adaptation rather than sudden shocks.

8.5.3.2 Governance Experimentation

Following Axelrod & Cohen's (2000) model of "complexity-aware institutions," DAOs can:

- Run pilot programs in sandbox environments to test novel governance tools (e.g., Aragon's dispute modules),
- Use iterative proposals to implement reform in stages and monitor outcomes.

8.5.3.3 Scenario Testing

Simulation tools, including agent-based models (ABMs), enable exploration of:

- Emergent behaviors under different governance regimes,
- Resilience under stress conditions (e.g., whale domination or participation collapse).

This kind of institutional modeling echoes Ostrom's (1990) emphasis on rules-in-use and contextual calibration.

8.5.3.4 Balancing Stability and Innovation

Overly stable DAOs risk stagnation or path dependence. Conversely, excessive innovation can fragment identity and erode trust.

- Mechanisms like meta-governance layers, constitutional amendments, or graduated experimentation offer ways to shift position across the fitness landscape without destabilizing the core institution.

The governance journey of a DAO, therefore, is not toward a single optimal solution, but through continuous realignment and navigation across a rugged and evolving terrain, where adaptive capacity becomes the cornerstone of sustainability.

8.6 Phase Transitions and Systemic Shifts

Phase transitions are critical phenomena observed in complex systems when small perturbations accumulate to trigger abrupt systemic change. As Waldrop (1992) explains, these transitions often occur at the "edge of chaos," a threshold region where systems shift between order and disorder. In institutional terms, these shifts resemble what Kauffman (1993) describes as "punctuated equilibria": long periods of stability disrupted by rapid transformation.

8.6.1 Concept of Phase Transitions

In the study of complex systems, phase transitions describe moments when a system rapidly reorganizes into a fundamentally different state. In physics, these range from melting solids to boiling liquids, each triggered by reaching a critical threshold. Governance systems, including DAOs, can experience similar tipping points, shifting from coherence to crisis due to accumulations of tension, narrative polarization, or external shocks.

In DAO ecosystems, such transitions often reflect:

- Shifts in consensus due to emerging ideological fractures,
- Crises of legitimacy triggered by external interventions,
- Structural reconfigurations following contentious governance votes or exploit events.

Recognizing these moments as systemic rather than incidental allows for the design of early-warning systems and crisis protocols that treat change not as failure, but as a phase in institutional evolution.

8.6.2 Indicators of Imminent Transitions

Complex systems approaching a phase transition often display early warning signals, patterns of increasing instability, volatility, or bifurcation, which complexity science identifies as critical slowing down or rising variance in system responses (Scheffer et al., 2009). In decentralized governance, similar indicators suggest a DAO may be nearing a structural rupture. Several early warning signals may suggest that a DAO is approaching a critical threshold:

- Voting pattern volatility: Sharp oscillations in vote margins, last-minute reversals, or dramatic changes in delegate alignment can indicate the breakdown of consensus heuristics and the rise of factionalization.

- Proposal proliferation: A sudden surge in conflicting or overlapping proposals may suggest the fragmentation of shared priorities and the loss of a coherent governance agenda.
- Narrative polarization: The emergence of competing ideological framings, often amplified by influential voices or media channels, signals a loss of common interpretive ground. Such polarization can crystallize along fault lines (e.g., "Code is Law" vs. "Human Intervention"), leading to hardened camps and zero-sum dynamics.

Detecting these signals in advance allows for preemptive action, be it through governance buffers, narrative mediation, or structural reform, aimed at averting uncontrolled transitions and preserving institutional coherence.

8.6.3 *Managing Phase Transitions*

Phase transitions cannot always be prevented, but their impact can be mitigated. In complexity theory, systems that survive turbulence often do so not by resisting change, but by absorbing shocks through redundancy, modularity, and flexible thresholds (Holland, 1992; Taleb, 2012). DAOs require similar design foresight.

8.6.3.1 Governance Buffers

Flexible parameters, such as dynamic quorum thresholds or staggered voting windows, act as buffers against volatility. They allow communities to modulate governance tempo in response to stress, creating space for deliberation without blocking responsiveness.

8.6.3.2 Emergency Procedures

While decentralization resists hierarchy, emergency protocols, temporarily granting multisig powers or activating delay mechanisms, can act as "governance circuit breakers." Crucially, these tools must include safeguards to prevent abuse, such as time-limited activation and community ratification.

8.6.3.3 Narrative Interventions

Beyond code, governance crises often hinge on meaning. Narrative interventions—calls for unity, clarification of mission, or appeals to shared identity—help reweave social cohesion. As March and Olsen (1984) noted, legitimacy is often restored not through rules, but through the reinterpretation of institutional purpose.

8.6.3.4 Case Example: Planned Vs. Traumatic Forks

A stark illustration of phase transitions in DAO ecosystems is the distinction between planned forks and traumatic forks.

- Planned forks: Occur through deliberate coordination and advance signaling. For example, in software projects, communities may amicably agree to diverge into separate versions, minimizing community damage.
- Traumatic forks: Erupt suddenly from irreconcilable conflicts, as with The DAO fork in 2016. The Ethereum community split into Ethereum and Ethereum Classic following a contentious debate about reversing the effects of a massive exploit. The lack of consensus and the rapid escalation of ideological divides transformed a governance dispute into a full-fledged systemic schism.

Understanding and preparing for such transitions is critical. While forks can be a legitimate tool for governance evolution, poorly managed transitions carry severe costs: loss of trust, fragmentation of communities, and diminished legitimacy.

Effective DAO design does not eliminate the possibility of phase transitions, it prepares for them. By embedding buffers, escalation pathways, and communicative scaffolds, decentralized systems can transform moments of rupture into catalysts for institutional renewal.

8.7 Implications for DAO Design: Building Institutions for Emergence and Adaption

8.7.1 Design Principles for Complexity

Traditional governance frameworks aim for optimization, clear rules, bounded procedures, and predictable outcomes. But in complexity-rich environments, optimization often fails. Instead, the challenge becomes one of evolvability: designing systems that do not collapse under uncertainty, but reorganize, learn, and adapt. In this context, DAO governance should not strive for perfection, but for resilience, modularity, and iterative refinement.

This section outlines design principles inspired by systems theory (Axelrod & Cohen, 2000; Holland, 1992) and institutional adaptability (March & Olsen, 1984; Ostrom, 1990), to support the development of robust and flexible decentralized governance.

Recognizing DAOs as CAS has profound implications for governance design. Traditional organizational models emphasize rigid structures, deterministic rules, and predictable cause-effect relationships. However, such approaches are often inadequate in decentralized contexts characterized by uncertainty, emergent behavior, and rapid environmental shifts.

Key principles for designing DAOs as CAS include:

- Modularity: Governance architectures should be structured in modular components, allowing parts of the system to evolve independently without destabilizing the whole. This reflects the principle of loose coupling in complex systems theory, where subsystems retain local autonomy while maintaining coherence through minimal yet strategic interconnections (Axelrod & Cohen, 2000). For instance:
  - SubDAOs with specialized mandates.
  - Working groups with autonomous decision-making but alignment to broader DAO goals.

- Error tolerance: Complex systems inevitably encounter unexpected shocks. DAO design should incorporate mechanisms to fail gracefully rather than catastrophically. This includes gradual rollouts of new features, controlled experimentation before full deployment, and redundancy in governance layers—similar to biological systems that rely on overlapping safeguards to prevent systemic collapse (Holland, 1992; Taleb, 2012). This includes:
  - Gradual rollouts of new features.
  - Controlled experimentation before full deployment.
  - Redundant systems to ensure continuity during failures.

- Adaptive governance: Governance systems must be capable of learning and adjusting. Fixed rules may become obsolete as circumstances change. Mechanisms such as meta-governance proposals, dynamic voting thresholds, or sunset clauses for new rules enable DAOs to evolve institutionally. This aligns with March and Olsen's (1984)

view of governance as a process of iterative learning, where structures are not merely implemented but continuously reinterpreted through practice. Examples of adaptive governance include:
– Meta-governance processes to revise institutional parameters.
– Dynamic quorum requirements adjusting to participation levels.

- Incorporating uncertainty as a feature: Uncertainty should not be seen merely as a threat to be neutralized, but as a generative condition for innovation. Embracing ambiguity through parallel proposal mechanisms, dissent-tolerant deliberation spaces, and iterative prototyping fosters institutional resilience. This resonates with Ostrom's (1990) principle of polycentric governance, where overlapping authorities and flexible boundaries allow experimentation without systemic collapse.

Designing DAOs for complexity does not mean abandoning structure; it means creating institutions that remain coherent under stress while retaining the capacity to evolve.

8.7.2 Practical Governance Tools

Translating complexity-informed principles into operational practice demands concrete governance tools, mechanisms that are not only theoretically grounded but contextually adaptable. These tools act as "bridging devices" (March & Olsen, 1984) between the uncertainty of decentralized environments and the need for coordination, learning, and institutional coherence.

8.7.2.1 Meta-Governance Frameworks

Meta-governance refers to governance mechanisms designed to change governance itself. Meta-governance has been theorized as a "governance of governance" (Jessop, 2003), enabling systems to adjust their own coordination mechanisms without external imposition. In DAOs, this means creating reflexive procedures that allow communities to adapt their structures over time, without undermining legitimacy or falling into ad hoc improvisation. It provides DAOs with:

- Protocols for updating governance rules.
- Processes for modifying voting systems, quorum thresholds, or delegate roles.
- Safeguards ensuring that changes are legitimate and not captured by special interests.

For example, Aragon's modular governance architecture allows DAOs to modify governance logic through meta-proposals, enabling evolution without hard forks.

8.7.2.2 Dynamic Quorum

Fixed quorum requirements often fail to reflect community dynamics. Dynamic quorum systems adjust thresholds based on factors like:

- Recent participation rates.
- Proposal significance or risk profile.
- Historical voting patterns.

This flexibility prevents governance paralysis during periods of low engagement and guards against hasty decisions during times of hyperactivity. Adaptive thresholds respond to what Ostrom (1990) called "situated rationality": the understanding that rules must emerge from, and be flexible to, specific contexts. Dynamic quorum mechanisms allow DAOs to mirror this principle by adjusting decision thresholds to reflect actual engagement and proposal significance.

8.7.2.3 Simulation Tools (Agent-Based Modeling)

DAO designers increasingly leverage ABM to simulate:

- How agents with diverse incentives behave under different governance rules.
- Emergent phenomena like voting cascades or coalition formation.
- System resilience under stress scenarios.

ABM enables DAO communities to test hypothetical changes without risking real-world assets, providing critical insights into potential unintended consequences.

The use of simulations reflects the broader institutional design principle advocated by March and Olsen (1984), in which decision processes must accommodate bounded rationality and institutional experimentation. ABM enables structured trial-and-error in silico, reducing real-world risk while preserving the adaptive ethos of decentralized governance.

For instance, MakerDAO researchers have used simulations to evaluate how parameter changes could affect liquidations and systemic stability.

8.7.3 Beyond Static Governance

The ultimate lesson from viewing DAOs as CAS is that governance should not be static, but continuously evolving. DAOs must be designed not as rigid machines executing immutable code, but as living institutions capable of learning, adapting, and regenerating.

This conception resonates with the institutional pluralism proposed by Scott (2008), in which the regulative, normative, and cultural-cognitive dimensions of institutions interact dynamically across time and context. DAOs embody all three: encoded rules (regulative), community values (normative), and emergent narratives (cultural-cognitive).

Similarly, Taleb's (2012) concept of "antifragility" reinforces the idea that decentralized systems should not merely survive disruption but improve through it. DAOs can become stronger after shocks, such as governance crises or forks, by transforming breakdowns into institutional learning opportunities.

Designing antifragile DAOs requires:

- Diversity of roles and perspectives,
- Embedded mechanisms for feedback and memory,
- Tolerance for experimentation and safe failure.

In this sense, DAO governance is less about eliminating uncertainty than about harnessing it as a resource for resilience. Complexity is not disorder—it is patterned unpredictability, and effective DAO design cultivates coherence within that fluidity.

8.8 Conclusion: Toward an Adaptive Institutional Theory

Throughout this chapter, we have demonstrated, drawing on complexity theory (Gell-Mann, 1994; Holland, 1992; Waldrop, 1992) and institutional analysis (March & Olsen, 1984; Ostrom, 1990; Scott, 2008), that

DAOs cannot be fully understood, nor effectively designed, through the lens of static protocols and deterministic governance. Instead, they must be viewed as CAS: living ecosystems where emergent behavior, non-linear dynamics, and adaptive learning shape governance outcomes far beyond the scope of code alone.

DAOs should be understood not as rigid, rule-bound protocols, but as adaptive institutional ecologies, shaped by feedback, contested meanings, and evolving governance dynamics.

This perspective fundamentally reframes our understanding of decentralized governance:

- It recognizes that rules and smart contracts are necessary but insufficient.
- It emphasizes that social dynamics, narratives, and emergent patterns are integral to how DAOs function and evolve.
- It accepts uncertainty and complexity as inherent, not as flaws to be eliminated.

8.8.1 Connection with Other Chapters

The insights from this chapter resonate deeply with concepts explored elsewhere in this book:

- Quantum governance: Both chapters highlight the limitations of deterministic models and stress the role of probabilistic reasoning, observer effects, and systemic interdependence in governance.
- Beyond the code: This chapter's focus on emergent behavior and institutional learning connects directly to discussions of the cultural, narrative, and behavioral dimensions of DAO governance. Governance is not simply what is written in code; it is a social and adaptive process.

Together, these perspectives build a holistic framework for understanding DAOs as institutional forms uniquely suited to complex, decentralized environments. This systems-oriented approach not only deepens theoretical insight but also grounds future design practices in the realities of adaptation, emergence, and collective learning.

8.8.2 *Directions for Future Research*

Despite advances in theoretical understanding, significant open questions remain for researchers and practitioners interested in developing resilient DAO governance.

- Empirical measurement of DAO complexity: How can we quantify emergent phenomena such as latent coordination, feedback loops, and phase transitions in real-world DAO ecosystems? Which indicators reliably signal systemic health or looming instability?
- Simulation and scenario testing: How can ABM and other simulation tools be used to anticipate unintended consequences of governance changes? What insights can we gain from stress-testing DAOs under hypothetical crisis scenarios?
- Design of resilient governance architectures: What practical design patterns best balance stability and innovation? How can DAOs remain adaptive without fragmenting into chaos during rapid environmental shifts?

Addressing these questions will require cross-disciplinary collaboration:

- Systems theory and complexity science.
- Network analysis and computational modeling.
- Legal theory and institutional economics.
- Behavioral psychology and organizational studies.

The path forward is challenging yet vital. As DAOs increasingly govern significant economic resources, social initiatives, and technological infrastructures, designing governance systems that embrace complexity, learn from experience, and remain resilient under stress is not merely an academic pursuit, it is an imperative for the sustainability of the decentralized ecosystem.

As the DAO ecosystem continues to mature, addressing these questions will require not only technical expertise but also cross-pollination between disciplines. Complexity theory, institutional design, behavioral economics, and computational sociology must converge to articulate an adaptive institutional theory capable of guiding the next generation of decentralized governance.

Toward an adaptive institutional theory, DAOs represent not just a technological innovation, but an evolutionary step in how human societies organize, deliberate, and decide.

8.9 Design Takeaways: DAO Governance Through the Lens of Decentralized Complexity

1. Governance as Emergent Ecology

DAO coordination evolves through distributed feedback loops, not top-down mandates. Emergent behaviors, not command protocols, drive systemic coherence.

2. Map the Fitness Landscape

Consider governance structures as navigating peaks and valleys: different configurations (protocol models, coordination tools) yield varying adaptability and resilience.

3. Enable Self-Organization and Reflexivity

Systems must adjust over time: DAO protocols should allow meta-governance and rule evolution in response to feedback and environmental change.

4. Design for Structural Diversity

Encourage multiple coordination modes (token, reputation, hybrid), similar to biological diversity, to avoid brittleness and enhance innovation.

5. Support Multiscale Institutional Learning

Mechanisms for memory and selective adaptation (accumulation of trust, archives, narratives) support long-term health, not just short-term efficiency.

By embracing complexity, DAOs shift from rigid governance blueprints to evolving institutional ecologies, capable of learning, adapting, and thriving amidst uncertainty. In this view, governance is not a finished product but a living process, shaped by interaction, iteration, and collective imagination.

References

Axelrod, R., & Cohen, M. D. (2000). *Harnessing complexity: Organizational implications of a scientific frontier*. Free Press.

Callon, M. (1998). *The laws of the markets*. Blackwell Publishers.

Gell-Mann, M. (1994). *The quark and the jaguar: Adventures in the simple and the complex*. W. H. Freeman.

Holland, J. H. (1992). *Adaptation in natural and artificial systems*. MIT Press.

Jessop, B. (2003). Governance and metagovernance: On reflexivity, requisite variety, and requisite irony. In H. Bang (Ed.), *Governance as social and political communication* (pp. 101–116). Manchester University Press.

Kauffman, S. A. (1993). *The origins of order: Self-organization and selection in evolution*. Oxford University Press.

March, J. G. (1991). Exploration and exploitation in organizational learning. *Organization science*, *2*(1), 71–87.

March, J. G., & Olsen, J. P. (1984). The new institutionalism: Organizational factors in political life. *American Political Science Review*, *78*(3), 734–749.

Ostrom, E. (1990). *Governing the commons: The evolution of institutions for collective action*. Cambridge University Press.

Scheffer, M., Bascompte, J., Brock, W. A., Brovkin, V., Carpenter, S. R., Dakos, V., Held, H., van Nes, E. H., Rietkerk, M., & Sugihara, G. (2009). Early-warning signals for critical transitions. *Nature*, *461*(7260), 53–59.

Scott, W. R. (2008). *Institutions and organizations: Ideas and interests*. Sage.

Taleb, N. N. (2012). *Antifragile: Things that gain from disorder*. Random House.

Tilly, C. (2005). *Trust and rule*. Cambridge University Press.

Waldrop, M. M. (1992). *Complexity: The emerging science at the edge of order and chaos*. Simon & Schuster.

CHAPTER 9

Governance or Mythology? Philosophical Paradoxes of Decentralization

9.1 Introduction

9.1.1 Beyond the Code: DAOs as Political and Cultural Constructs

Decentralized autonomous organizations (DAOs) are often described as purely technical innovations, systems of smart contracts, token-based voting, and automated governance. Yet, this vision captures only part of the truth. DAOs are political and cultural constructs as much as they are technical architectures.

At their core, DAOs encode not merely operational rules but normative frameworks, visions of fairness, and collective identities. They become arenas where competing values, ideologies, and social imaginaries are negotiated. Behind the neutrality of "code" lie assumptions about human behavior, power distribution, and the legitimacy of decisions.

DAOs thus represent a paradox: they promise to replace the subjectivity of human institutions with algorithmic objectivity, yet they inevitably replicate or reinvent the same political tensions, social hierarchies, and cultural rituals found in traditional organizations.

Understanding DAOs requires moving beyond purely technical analysis and confronting them as emerging institutional forms that exist at the intersection of politics, culture, and technology.

A. Cesaretti, *DAO Governance in Theory and Practice*,
https://doi.org/10.1007/978-3-032-09675-3_9

9.1.2 The Need for a Meta-institutional Analysis

To analyze DAOs purely through the lens of code or economic efficiency is insufficient. What is needed is a meta-institutional perspective, an approach that examines not just how DAOs function internally, but how they produce meaning, construct legitimacy, and shape social relations.

Such an analysis must engage with questions like:

- How do DAOs establish legitimacy in the absence of electoral systems or traditional legal structures?
- To what extent does "decentralization" actually distribute power, rather than merely displace it?
- What myths, narratives, or charismatic figures sustain DAOs as communities, not just protocols?

DAOs do not simply execute rules; they generate symbols, rituals, and ideological claims. This symbolic layer can become a source of cohesion, but also a source of manipulation or ideological capture.

This chapter aims to uncover the philosophical and political undercurrents of decentralized governance. It explores how DAOs oscillate between being institutions of collective self-determination and mythologies that promise salvation from the failures of traditional governance, yet sometimes reproduce the same pathologies in new forms.

Rather than offering prescriptive answers, the chapter invites readers into a critical reflection on the paradoxes and tensions embedded in the mythology and reality of decentralization.

9.2 The DAO as a Political Form

9.2.1 Decentralization as a Paradigm of Self-governance

At its core, decentralization in the context of DAOs aspires to implement a paradigm of self-governance, wherein authority and decision-making are distributed among network participants rather than concentrated in hierarchical leadership structures. This ideal is grounded in the conviction that trust can be shifted from institutions and individuals to protocols and cryptographic guarantees.

Decentralization, however, is not merely a technical architecture; it represents a profound political claim: that collective coordination can emerge spontaneously, sustained by incentives, transparent processes, and shared norms, rather than imposed by external authorities. This vision resonates with classical liberal theories of spontaneous order, yet diverges in its reliance on programmable rules rather than unwritten conventions.

Nevertheless, the practical implementation of decentralized governance reveals inherent tensions. Protocols designed to distribute power often reproduce asymmetries:

- Influence is frequently consolidated in the hands of token-rich actors ("whales").
- Participation rates vary, leading to governance captured by small minorities.
- Technical complexity creates new barriers to meaningful engagement.

Thus, while decentralization aspires to democratize governance, it must confront the paradox of decentralization: the possibility that networks nominally designed to eliminate central authority may, in practice, engender new forms of concentrated influence and invisible hierarchies.

9.2.2 *Between Community, Enterprise, Institution, and Proto-state*

DAOs defy traditional classificatory boundaries. They are simultaneously:

- Communities, built on shared identities, narratives, and cultural symbols.
- Enterprises, managing financial resources, deploying capital, and generating economic value.
- Institutions, establishing procedural norms and dispute resolution mechanisms.
- Proto-states, in some cases, wielding quasi-sovereign powers, setting rules for their ecosystem, and administering treasuries that rival national budgets.

This hybrid character complicates analytical efforts. For instance:

- As communities, DAOs cultivate belonging and meaning, drawing members who identify with their mission beyond economic gain. Yet community dynamics can foster tribalism and exclusion.

- As enterprises, DAOs pursue efficiency and profitability but face unique challenges in aligning decentralized decision-making with coherent strategic direction.
- As institutions, DAOs aspire to durability and legitimacy, but lack established mechanisms for legal accountability and enforcement.
- As proto-states, certain DAOs, particularly those governing critical DeFi infrastructure, exercise regulatory-like powers without being subject to democratic oversight or legal jurisdiction.

These overlapping identities create profound ambiguity. They also generate jurisdictional and normative challenges:

- How should regulators classify DAOs, as associations, corporations, or autonomous collectives?
- To whom are DAOs accountable when they cross national boundaries?
- What legal personhood, if any, should be attributed to decentralized networks?

Understanding DAOs as political forms thus requires transcending binary categories and embracing their polycentric, fluid nature. They are institutions in motion, simultaneously social, economic, and political constructs.

9.2.3 *The Problem of Legitimacy in Non-electoral Systems*

One of the most pressing philosophical and practical challenges confronting DAOs is the problem of legitimacy. Unlike traditional democratic institutions, DAOs do not derive authority from electoral mandates, territorial jurisdiction, or constitutional frameworks. Instead, their legitimacy is grounded in:

- Procedural transparency (the idea that open rules generate trust).
- Participatory rhetoric (the claim that all stakeholders can influence outcomes).
- Technological neutrality (the belief that code enforces fairness without human bias).

However, these sources of legitimacy are neither stable nor uncontested. Several key issues arise:

- Participation asymmetry: While DAOs claim inclusiveness, active governance often involves a minority of highly engaged actors, leaving silent majorities effectively disenfranchised.
- Token-weighted voting: Governance power correlates with token holdings, introducing plutocratic tendencies. Wealth becomes a proxy for political influence, raising questions of justice and representativeness.
- Narrative legitimacy: DAOs frequently rely on foundational myths, charismatic founders, or ideological slogans ("community-led," "decentralized governance") to secure loyalty. Yet these narratives can obscure power imbalances or mask centralized decision-making.

Moreover, legitimacy in DAOs remains fragile because it is:

- Disconnected from formal legal systems.
- Subject to rapid shifts in sentiment.
- Dependent on the continued engagement of participants.

In the absence of traditional institutional guarantees, DAOs must continually reproduce legitimacy through transparent processes, meaningful participation, and effective communication. Failure to do so risks governance crises, community fragmentation, or even existential splits (as seen in notable forks like Ethereum vs. Ethereum Classic).

Ultimately, the question persists: Can DAOs establish durable legitimacy without replicating the very institutional structures they sought to transcend? This remains one of the central paradoxes of decentralized governance.

9.3 Three Theoretical Visions: Hayek, Rawls, Foucault

The following section engages three theoretical traditions not as endorsements, but as interpretive lenses to interrogate the layered nature of decentralized governance.

The philosophical and political analysis of DAOs benefits from engaging with diverse intellectual traditions. In this chapter, we draw upon the insights of three major thinkers:

- Friedrich August von Hayek (1899–1992), an Austrian economist and social theorist associated with classical liberalism and the Austrian School of Economics, best known for his theory of spontaneous order and critique of central planning.
- John Rawls (1921–2002), an American political philosopher and a leading figure in liberal political theory, whose work on justice as fairness established foundational principles for procedural legitimacy and distributive justice.
- Michel Foucault (1926–1984), a French philosopher and social theorist, known for his analyses of power, knowledge, and governance, and for revealing how invisible structures and discourses shape social and institutional behavior.

Each offers a distinct lens for interrogating the paradoxes of decentralized governance:

- Hayek emphasizes emergent order through decentralized interactions.
- Rawls focuses on procedural fairness and justice.
- Foucault unveils the subtle, invisible mechanisms through which power operates even in seemingly decentralized systems.

Together, their theories provide a rich framework for understanding DAOs not merely as technical systems, but as political, cultural, and ethical institutions.

9.3.1 Hayek and Spontaneous Order: Trust in Algorithmic Catallaxy

Friedrich August von Hayek's theory of spontaneous order (Hayek, 1945, 1960) posits that complex social coordination arises not from central planning but from decentralized interactions among individuals, each acting on local knowledge and personal incentives. Markets, in this view, function as information-processing mechanisms that aggregate dispersed knowledge, producing efficient outcomes without central direction.

This vision resonates profoundly with the ethos of DAOs. The blockchain ecosystem often frames itself as an algorithmic catallaxy:

- Protocols replace bureaucratic institutions.
- Price signals and token incentives coordinate behavior.
- Governance emerges from voluntary actions rather than imposed authority.

In DAOs, smart contracts become the digital infrastructure of spontaneous order, enabling trustless interactions without intermediaries. The rhetoric suggests that:

- Code ensures impartial rule enforcement.
- Incentive structures align individual self-interest with collective welfare.

Yet, critical differences exist between Hayek's spontaneous order and DAO governance:

- Transparency vs. opacity: While blockchain is transparent, the complexity of smart contracts and governance structures can obscure rather than reveal information to non-technical participants.
- Local knowledge vs. global protocols: Hayek emphasizes local, tacit knowledge, whereas DAOs often impose globally uniform rules, potentially suppressing contextual nuance.
- Emergent order vs. engineered incentives: Hayek's spontaneous order arises organically, while DAOs frequently rely on deliberately designed incentive architectures, raising questions about who designs these systems and whose interests they serve.

Thus, while Hayek's framework offers a compelling justification for decentralized coordination, its application to DAOs reveals tensions between emergent order and the engineering of social behavior via algorithmic governance.

9.3.2 Rawls and Procedural Justice: Voting, Fairness, and Information Asymmetries

John Rawls, in his theory of justice as fairness (Rawls, 1971), emphasizes procedural justice as a cornerstone of legitimate institutions. Rules are considered just if they would be chosen behind a "veil of ignorance," where no one knows their position or advantage in society. This principle prioritizes:

- Equal basic liberties.
- Fair equality of opportunity.
- Attention to the welfare of the least advantaged.

DAOs frequently invoke procedural ideals:

- Transparent voting processes.
- Public discussion forums.
- Immutable on-chain records.

Superficially, these mechanisms appear aligned with Rawlsian principles. However, significant discrepancies emerge:

- Token-weighted voting contradicts Rawls' egalitarian ethos. In most DAOs, political power scales with token ownership, creating plutocratic tendencies where wealth equates to governance influence.
- Information asymmetries persist. Technically sophisticated actors can exploit complex protocols, while ordinary participants lack the resources or expertise to fully engage. This violates Rawls' condition that institutions should be designed from a standpoint of equal knowledge.
- Procedural legitimacy vs. substantive fairness: Even if processes are transparent, outcomes may still systematically disadvantage certain participants, challenging Rawls' insistence on protecting the least advantaged.

Thus, while DAOs strive for procedural legitimacy, they often fall short of achieving the substantive fairness central to Rawlsian justice. The paradox is that decentralized governance, in seeking to democratize participation, may inadvertently replicate or exacerbate existing social and economic inequalities.

9.3.3 *Foucault and Invisible Power: Governance as Behavioral Design*

Michel Foucault's analyses of power (Foucault, 1977, 1991) challenge the notion that authority resides only in visible institutions, laws, or formal structures. Instead, power often operates through invisible mechanisms:

- Disciplinary techniques.
- Normative discourses.
- Knowledge regimes that shape what is perceived as true or legitimate.

In the context of DAOs, Foucault's insights reveal that decentralization does not eliminate power; it merely reconfigures its modalities:

- Protocol design as a form of governance: Smart contracts encode rules that shape participant behavior, deciding what is possible, permissible, or incentivized.
- Normative narratives: Rhetoric around "community," "transparency," and "trustlessness" serves as a powerful ideological framework, guiding expectations and suppressing dissent.
- Data-driven behavioral nudging: Governance mechanisms often incorporate reputation systems, voting incentives, and other feedback loops that subtly steer participation and align behavior with protocol objectives.

DAOs thus exemplify Foucault's concept of governmentality, the exercise of power not through overt coercion, but through the structuring of the field of possible actions:

- Governance becomes behavioral design, where the true authority lies not in visible governance votes but in the invisible architecture of incentives, interfaces, and social signaling.
- Participants may believe themselves autonomous, yet their actions are channeled and normalized by systems designed to produce specific outcomes.

This Foucauldian perspective compels a critical interrogation of DAOs:

- Who designs these governance mechanisms?
- Whose interests do they serve?
- How do they shape, constrain, or enable genuine autonomy and collective self-determination?

Decentralized systems, rather than escaping power dynamics, may therefore reinvent subtle architectures of control, raising crucial ethical and political questions about the opacity of algorithmic governance and the legitimacy of invisible authority

9.4 Is Code Law? Epistemology, Authority, and Contestability

9.4.1 *Code as Norm: Between Automation and Legitimacy*

The aphorism "Code is Law", popularized in the early blockchain movement, encapsulates the belief that programmable protocols can replace traditional legal and institutional structures. In this vision, rules are no longer subject to interpretation, discretion, or political capture; instead, they are executed automatically and deterministically by smart contracts. The notion of "Code is Law", as originally articulated by Buterin (2014), defines the shift from legal to algorithmic governance in blockchain systems. This dynamic reflects what Yeung and Lodge (2019) describe as "algorithmic regulation", where computational systems substitute formalized procedures for human deliberation.

However, code as law is not merely a technical proposition, it is a normative claim. It asserts:

- That legitimacy arises from formal consistency and technical transparency.
- That human judgment is inherently unreliable, whereas code offers incorruptible objectivity.

Yet, several tensions complicate this narrative:

- Semantic opacity: Smart contracts may be transparent in code, but their functional implications are often inaccessible to non-technical participants, undermining true procedural legitimacy.
- Ambiguity and context: Rules encoded in code cannot anticipate every possible scenario. They lack the capacity for interpretation, equity, and context-sensitive judgment that legal systems traditionally provide.

- Social legitimacy: Even perfectly executed code may fail to command legitimacy if it produces outcomes perceived as unfair, unreasonable, or contrary to community values.

Thus, while code enforces rules with precision, it cannot substitute for the normative processes through which societies negotiate legitimacy, fairness, and ethical acceptability. Governance, even in DAOs, remains a hybrid enterprise. part algorithmic, part interpretive.

9.4.2 Popper and the Falsifiability of On-Chain Governance

Karl Popper (1902–1994) was an Austrian-British philosopher of science, renowned for his theory of falsifiability as the criterion distinguishing scientific knowledge from dogma. According to Popper, a theory is scientific only if it can, in principle, be proven false through empirical testing. Systems that cannot admit the possibility of error or revision are not open systems of knowledge but closed ideological constructs.

Popper's insights extend beyond scientific methodology to democratic theory and institutional design. He argued that robust societies and institutions must:

- Allow for criticism and contestation.
- Be capable of correcting mistakes without resorting to violent upheaval.
- Remain open to new information and adaptive learning.

In the context of decentralized governance, Popper's philosophy provides a powerful lens for assessing whether DAOs:

- Enable critical feedback.
- Incorporate mechanisms for revising flawed rules.
- Remain flexible in the face of unforeseen challenges.

Karl Popper's epistemological principle of falsifiability (Popper, 1959, 1963) holds that scientific theories must be structured such that they can, in principle, be proven wrong. A system that cannot admit the possibility of its own error is not scientific but dogmatic.

Applying this insight to DAO governance reveals profound implications:

- Infallibility vs. adaptability: Smart contracts execute rules exactly as written. However, this very determinism can become a liability if rules prove inadequate or harmful under unforeseen circumstances.
- Lack of contestability: In many DAOs, once code is deployed, there exists no built-in process for challenging or revising outcomes other than proposing new code. This rigidity risks transforming governance into an uncontestable formalism, violating Popper's principle that systems must remain open to criticism and correction.
- Edge cases and black swans: Governance crises, security exploits, or shifts in community values often expose blind spots in protocols. Without mechanisms for reflexivity and contestation, DAOs risk institutional fragility.

Popper's framework suggests that DAOs should not aspire to infallibility, but rather to structures that:

- Enable iterative learning.
- Allow for procedural contestation.
- Integrate community feedback as a mechanism for self-correction.

The paradox is clear: code promises certainty, but sustainable governance requires institutionalized doubt and pathways for deliberate change.

9.4.3 The Risk of Technical Infallibility and Missing Feedback Loops

One of the most seductive myths in decentralized systems is that technical infallibility guarantees social legitimacy. The assumption is that if code functions correctly, governance is necessarily fair and just. However, this belief obscures several critical risks:

- Feedback blindness: Algorithms cannot perceive shifts in community sentiment, evolving norms, or moral considerations unless explicitly coded to do so. Systems that lack feedback loops are vulnerable to becoming disconnected from the communities they govern.

- Immutability as rigidity: While immutability is a cornerstone of blockchain security, it can become a liability when circumstances change. Protocols that cannot adapt may preserve flawed rules long after their utility has vanished.
- Disempowerment of participants: Over-reliance on "code as law" can marginalize participants, reducing governance to technical priesthoods where only a few possess the expertise to influence or revise protocols.
- Narrative legitimacy vs. procedural infallibility: DAOs often sustain themselves through symbolic narratives about fairness, openness, and community sovereignty. When technical rules produce outcomes that conflict with these narratives, a crisis of legitimacy ensues.

Historical examples abound:

- The DAO hack of 2016 revealed the tension between immutable code and collective values, leading to the Ethereum/Ethereum Classic split.
- Protocol forks often emerge when communities reject technically correct but socially unacceptable outcomes. As Taleb (2012) observes systems that embrace volatility and uncertainty can become "antifragile", learning from shocks instead of collapsing.

Sustainable governance in DAOs thus requires:

- Building adaptive feedback loops that connect technical systems to human values.
- Designing institutions capable of integrating dissent and contestation.
- Recognizing that no technical architecture, however elegant, can fully replace the messy, interpretive work of political and ethical deliberation.

In short, while technical precision is essential, governance without contestability and feedback risks transforming decentralized systems into rigid, self-referential machines—incapable of recognizing their own failures.

9.5 Myths, Symbols, and Charisma: The Religious Layer of Decentralization

9.5.1 The Founder as a Charismatic Figure (Weber)

Max Weber (1864–1920) was a German sociologist and political economist, renowned for his analyses of authority, bureaucracy, and the role of ideas in shaping social structures. Among his most influential concepts is the notion of charismatic authority (Weber, 1922), a form of legitimacy derived not from legal norms or traditional institutions, but from the personal qualities and perceived extraordinary gifts of an individual leader.

In the context of DAOs, Weber's concept of charisma offers a critical lens through which to understand:

- The founder figure as both visionary and symbol.
- The tendency of decentralized communities to gravitate toward personalities who embody the mission or myth of the project.
- The tension between charisma and the ethos of decentralization.

DAOs ostensibly reject central leadership, aspiring to create trustless systems governed by code. Yet, paradoxically, many DAOs remain deeply influenced by founders whose reputations and narratives:

- Shape community identity.
- Legitimize protocol decisions.
- Anchor ideological cohesion.

Examples abound:

- Vitalik Buterin's symbolic role within the Ethereum ecosystem.
- The mystique surrounding Satoshi Nakamoto as the absent, quasi-messianic figure in Bitcoin's narrative.
- Prominent DeFi project leaders whose endorsements can sway governance outcomes and market sentiment.

Weber warns that while charismatic authority can catalyze social movements, it also carries risks:

- Personal loyalty can overshadow institutional mechanisms.
- Communities may suppress dissent to preserve the leader's image.
- The transition from charismatic to rational-legal authority is fraught, risking fragmentation if the charismatic figure departs.

Thus, even in ostensibly leaderless DAOs, the figure of the founder often becomes a focal point of myth and symbolic power, revealing the persistent human tendency to seek meaning and legitimacy in charismatic leadership.

9.5.2 *Liberation Narratives: Between Technological Eschatology and the Cult of Immutability*

The language surrounding decentralized technology often carries eschatological undertones, grand narratives about liberation, salvation, and the overthrow of corrupt institutions. DAOs are not merely technical innovations; they are myth-making engines that promise:

- The end of traditional intermediaries.
- The democratization of finance and governance.
- The birth of new forms of community and economic freedom.

Such narratives frequently mirror religious structures:

- Prophetic figures announcing a transformative future.
- Sacred texts in the form of whitepapers.
- Rituals of initiation, including token launches and governance votes.

A central theme is the cult of immutability:

- Immutability is hailed as the ultimate guarantee of fairness and incorruptibility.
- Smart contracts are revered as infallible mechanisms of justice.

Yet, these beliefs harbor contradictions:

- Immutability can preserve unjust or flawed rules, preventing necessary adaptations.
- Technological determinism risks overshadowing the political, social, and ethical complexities of governance.
- Faith in code can morph into dogma, resistant to criticism or reform.

The danger lies in substituting critical reflection with quasi-religious adherence to technological solutions. Liberation narratives can motivate participation and solidarity, but they can also foster ideological rigidity, suppressing debate and masking new forms of power concentration.

9.5.3 *Governance Washing and the Dangers of Decentralization as Ideology*

Just as corporations have engaged in "greenwashing", superficial environmental commitments masking unsustainable practices, some projects engage in "governance washing." They adopt the language of decentralization, while maintaining:

- Centralized control over treasury funds.
- Opaque decision-making structures.
- Undisclosed influence by founding teams or venture capital stakeholders.

This dissonance between rhetoric and reality creates significant risks:

- Participants may be misled into believing they possess genuine agency.
- Centralized actors may exploit the legitimacy of "decentralization" for private gain.
- Critical scrutiny is muted by ideological narratives portraying any dissent as disloyalty.

Decentralization, when treated as pure ideology, becomes:

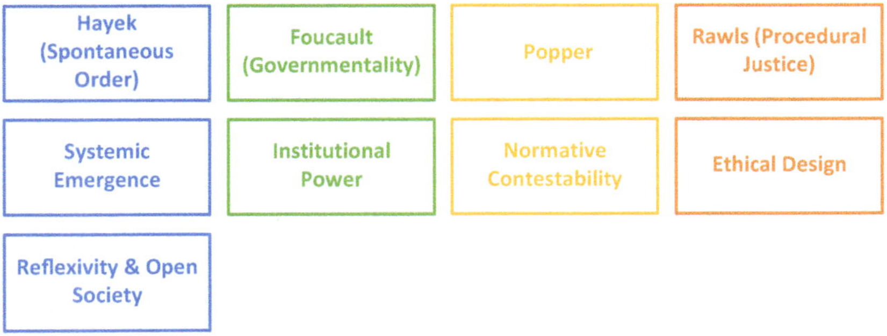

Fig. 9.1 Philosophical Foundations of Decentralized Governance. The figure maps key intellectual lineages that shape decentralized governance, including Foucault's critique of invisible power. These frameworks inform the ethical, political, and epistemological layers of DAO governance

- A moral signifier rather than a measurable institutional reality.
- A shield against accountability, as criticisms are dismissed as attacks on community values.
- A source of "narrative capture," where projects sustain legitimacy not through democratic processes but through compelling storytelling.

Foucault's notion of invisible power resurfaces here: decentralized systems can conceal new hierarchies behind the rhetoric of openness and participation. Governance washing erodes trust, undermines the legitimacy of authentic decentralized initiatives, and threatens to reduce the promise of DAOs to mere mythological branding.

To preserve the transformative potential of decentralized governance, communities must:

- Demand transparency about decision-making structures.
- Critically interrogate who holds influence and how power operates.
- Resist the allure of ideological comfort in favor of rigorous institutional design and accountability (Fig. 9.1)

9.6 Toward a Civic Theology of DAOs?

9.6.1 *The Need for Shared Values Beyond Ideological Dogma*

As DAOs evolve from technical experiments to significant socio-economic institutions, they confront a fundamental question: Can decentralized systems sustain legitimacy and cohesion without shared values?

While decentralization is often celebrated as an antidote to hierarchical authority and institutional corruption, it risks devolving into ideological dogma when it substitutes technical mechanisms for ethical deliberation. Phrases like "code is law" can obscure:

- Moral complexities in governance decisions.
- The need for compassion and equity.
- The unavoidable presence of power dynamics even in decentralized systems.

A purely procedural approach, no matter how elegant, is insufficient. Governance systems require:

- Normative foundations to navigate conflicts.
- Shared understandings of fairness, justice, and communal purpose.
- Cultural frameworks that transform participation into collective stewardship rather than mere transactional engagement.

Without such foundations, DAOs risk becoming empty shells, technically sophisticated but socially fragile, vulnerable to manipulation, apathy, or ideological capture.

9.6.2 *Education for Participation, Not Worship of Infrastructure*

Decentralization movements often emphasize technical literacy and the transparency of code. However, effective participation in DAO governance requires more than understanding smart contracts or token mechanics. It demands:

- Critical political literacy: The capacity to interrogate narratives, challenge authority, and evaluate competing visions of governance.

- Ethical reasoning: The ability to deliberate on questions of justice, equity, and the common good.
- Narrative competence: Understanding how symbols and stories shape collective action and institutional memory.

Too often, decentralized communities cultivate a worship of infrastructure, an almost religious reverence for protocols, cryptographic guarantees, and immutable ledgers. This technocratic mindset risks:

- Marginalizing dissent as heresy.
- Obscuring the human dimensions of governance.
- Conflating technical correctness with moral legitimacy.

A truly participatory DAO ecosystem requires education as empowerment:

- Members must be equipped to read both the code and the narratives that structure power.
- Communities should foster debate, pluralism, and reflexivity rather than uniformity of belief.

Only then can DAOs realize their potential as civic institutions, rather than remaining enclaves of technical elitism or ideological orthodoxy.

9.6.3 Building Sustainable Legitimacy Across Code, Community, and Culture

Legitimacy in DAOs is a multidimensional construct, arising not solely from technical mechanisms but from the interplay of:

- Code: Rules encoded in smart contracts, providing transparency and predictability.
- Community: The social layer that interprets rules, mediates conflicts, and sustains collective identity.
- Culture: The shared narratives, values, and symbols that give meaning to collective action.

Sustainable governance requires weaving these threads into a cohesive institutional fabric. Challenges include:

- Bridging gaps between technically sophisticated participants and broader communities.
- Maintaining institutional memory to avoid repeating past mistakes.
- Balancing openness to dissent with the need for stability and coherence.

The notion of a "civic theology" for DAOs does not imply importing metaphysical or religious doctrines into governance. Rather, it suggests:

- Recognizing the symbolic and normative dimensions inherent in any institutional framework.
- Consciously designing rituals, narratives, and communicative practices that foster trust, transparency, and mutual accountability.
- Embedding shared values that transcend purely technical definitions of decentralization.

DAOs, if they aspire to be more than financial instruments or ideological experiments, must cultivate institutional cultures that integrate code, community, and culture into a resilient and adaptive whole. Only then can they evolve into normative laboratories of the twenty-first century, capable of balancing innovation with ethical responsibility.

9.7 Conclusion

9.7.1 DAOs as Normative Laboratories of the Twenty-first Century

Throughout this chapter, we have explored how DAOs transcend their identity as purely technical systems, emerging instead as normative laboratories where new forms of governance, legitimacy, and social coordination are being actively experimented. DAOs are not merely digital organizations; they represent:

- Political experiments, testing alternative models of decision-making and collective action.

- Cultural projects, constructing identities, narratives, and symbolic universes.
- Institutional prototypes, seeking to redefine how communities organize, allocate resources, and resolve conflicts.

Their significance lies not only in their technological innovations but in their capacity to provoke fundamental questions about power, justice, and institutional design:

- Can governance be fully automated without sacrificing human judgment and ethical deliberation?
- How can systems ensure fairness while operating under conditions of radical decentralization?
- To what extent do narratives and symbolic structures influence institutional stability and community cohesion?

In positioning DAOs as normative laboratories, we recognize that they:

- Reveal both the possibilities and limitations of algorithmic governance.
- Illuminate enduring tensions between autonomy and control, transparency and opacity, and participation and expertise.
- Serve as crucibles where theoretical principles are tested under real-world constraints.

Thus, DAOs constitute critical spaces for reimagining institutional architectures in the twenty-first century, a domain where political theory, technology, and social imagination converge.

9.7.2 *From Mythology to Design: Beyond Rhetoric, Toward Collective Responsibility*

The discourse around decentralization often oscillates between mythology and pragmatism. On one hand, there is:

- Mythological rhetoric, portraying DAOs as instruments of liberation, incorruptibility, and perfect fairness.
- Symbolic narratives that sustain community identity but risk obscuring real power dynamics.

On the other hand, there is the pragmatic necessity of institutional design, which demands:

- Acknowledging the persistence of power, even in decentralized systems.
- Crafting governance mechanisms that balance efficiency, fairness, and adaptability.
- Cultivating cultures of accountability and critical participation.

Transitioning from mythology to design requires:

- Institutional humility: Recognizing that no protocol can capture all social complexities or eliminate uncertainty.
- Critical reflexivity: Continuously questioning narratives, authority structures, and systemic biases.
- Collective responsibility: Embracing governance not merely as rule execution but as a shared ethical endeavor.

DAOs must avoid becoming technocratic utopias disconnected from the lived experiences of their participants. Instead, they should aspire to become:

- Institutions capable of integrating technical innovation with social and cultural meaning.
- Platforms for genuine deliberation and adaptive learning.
- Spaces where collective intelligence is harnessed to navigate complexity rather than suppressed under rigid dogma.

Ultimately, the path forward for DAOs lies not in abandoning their transformative ambitions, but in grounding those ambitions in conscious design, ethical reflection, and participatory stewardship. Only then can decentralized governance move beyond myth into the realm of sustainable, responsible institutional innovation.

In the end, the most radical promise of decentralized governance is not its rejection of power, but its capacity to transform power into shared responsibility, narrative into deliberation, and protocol into living institution.

9.8 Design Takeaways: Governance as Critical, Civic, and Narrative Practice

1. Narrative is Infrastructure

Governance legitimacy does not derive solely from code or voting procedures, but from the shared narratives that sustain collective identity, memory, and purpose.

2. Power is Inevitable. Make it Accountable

Even in decentralized systems, power emerges. The goaln is not its elimination but its visibility, contestability, and ethical redistribution.

3. Reflexivity Over Formalism

No governance model is complete or self-justifying. Sustainable DAOs embrace iterative reform, critical introspection, and openness to revision.

4. Design with Civic Humility

DAO architects must acknowledge the normative implications of their choices. Rules are not neutral; they embed visions of justice, participation, and inclusion.

5. From Myth to Method

Myths can inspire action, but must be translated into design principles, institutional safeguards, and community practices to avoid becoming ideology.

References

Buterin, V. (2014). *DAOs, DACs, DAs and More: An incomplete terminology guide*. Ethereum Blog. Retrieved, from https://blog.ethereum.org
Foucault, M. (1977). *Discipline and punish: The birth of the prison*. Pantheon Books.

Foucault, M. (1991). Governmentality. In G. Burchell, C. Gordon, & P. Miller (Eds.), *The foucault effect: Studies in governmentality* (pp. 87–104). University of Chicago Press.

Hayek, F. A. (1945). The use of knowledge in society. *American Economic Review*, *35*(4), 519–530.

Hayek, F. A. (1960). *The constitution of liberty*. University of Chicago Press.

Popper, K. (1959). *The logic of scientific discovery*. Hutchinson.

Popper, K. (1963). *Conjectures and refutations: The growth of scientific knowledge*. Routledge.

Rawls, J. (1971). *A theory of justice*. Harvard University Press.

Taleb, N. N. (2012). *Antifragile: Things that gain from disorder*. Random House.

Weber, M. (1922). *Economy and society: An outline of interpretive sociology*. University of California Press.

Yeung, K., & Lodge, M. (2019). Algorithmic regulation. *Regulation & Governance*, *13*(1), 1–13.

Index

A. Cesaretti, *DAO Governance in Theory and Practice*,
https://doi.org/10.1007/978-3-032-09675-3

FSC
www.fsc.org
MIX
Papier | Fördert
gute Waldnutzung
FSC® C083411

Kolibri 360 GmbH
Ferdinand-Jühlke-Straße 7
99095 Erfurt, Deutschland
produktsicherheit@kolibri360.de